CONCELEBRATION OF MASS
AND
COMMUNION UNDER BOTH SPECIES

PIERRE JOUNEL

THE RITE
OF CONCELEBRATION
OF MASS
AND OF COMMUNION
UNDER BOTH SPECIES

History - Texts in English and Commentaries

DESCLEE COMPANY

NEW YORK - ROME - TOURNAI - PARIS

Originally published in French with the collaboration of the *Centre National de Pastorale Liturgique* in Paris, under the title *La Concélébration* © 1966 by Desclée & Cie, Paris.

This English edition © 1967 by Desclee Co. Inc., New York.

Library of Congress Catalog Card Number: 67-17679.

Printed and bound in Belgium by Desclée & Cie, Éditeurs S. A., Tournai.

Nihil obstat

J. Roussel, can., libr. cens.

Imprimatur

Tornaci, die 25 februarii 1967

J. Thomas, vic. gen.

TABLE OF CONTENTS

1

CONCELEBRATION OF THE MASS AND COMMUNION UNDER BOTH SPECIES THROUGHOUT THE CENTURIES

Introduction 9

Chapter I. History of Eucharistic Concelebration 13
  1. Concelebration in the Early Church 13
  2. Concelebration in the Eastern Churches 16
  3. Concelebration in the Roman Church 19

Chapter II. Concelebration at the Second Vatican Council . . 25
  1. The Problem of Concelebration in 1959 25
  2. The Council's Constitution 29

Chapter III. The New Ritual of Concelebration 35

Chapter IV. Communion under Both Species 45
  1. History of the Rite of Communion 45
  2. Communion under Both Species at the Second Vatican Council 61

2

THE RITE TO BE OBSERVED IN THE CONCELEBRATION OF MASS AND THE RITE OF COMMUNION UNDER BOTH SPECIES

General Decree 71

Rite to be Observed in Concelebration of Mass 77
  Preliminary Observations 77
  Rite for the Pontifical Mass 108

Rite of the Solemn Mass 138

Rite of the Mass with a Deacon 142

Rite of the Sung Mass 143

Rite of the Recited Mass 147

Concelebration of Mass in which Ordination to the
    Priesthood is Conferred 152

Concelebration of Mass in which Episcopal Consecration
    is Conferred 157

Concelebration of Mass in which an Abbot is Blessed . 163

Rite of Concelebration for Priests who are Infirm . . 166

*Rite to be Observed in the Distribution of Communion under Both
Species*

Preliminary Observations 169

1. Rite of Communion under Both Species when the
    Communicants Drink from the Chalice Itself . . 179

2. Rite of Communion under Both Species by Intinction . 182

3. Rite of Communion under Both Species with a Straw . 183

4. Rite of Communion under Both Species with a Spoon . 185

3

CANON OF THE MASS FOR CONCELEBRATION 187

I

CONCELEBRATION OF THE MASS
AND COMMUNION
UNDER BOTH SPECIES
THROUGHOUT THE CENTURIES

Introduction

Socia exsultatione concelebrant : every day the word " concelebrate " resounds in the Roman Liturgy. It is said of
the praise which the blessed spirits lift to heaven toward
the Divine Majesty. To this angelic concelebration, the
Church on earth joins its voice in singing the *Sanctus* and
in offering the Eucharistic Sacrifice.

HIERARCHICAL CONCELEBRATION

The whole liturgy is a concelebration. The Second
Vatican Council teaches that " liturgical services are not
private functions, but are celebrations of the Church,
which is the ' sacrament of unity, ' namely, the holy
people united and ordered under their Bishops. Therefore
liturgical services pertain to the whole body of the Church;
they manifest it and have effects upon it; but they concern
the individual members of the Church in different ways,
according to their differing rank, office, and actual participation " (C 26). In this perspective, every liturgical
action which receives its organic development constitutes
a communal and hierarchic celebration; it is a concelebration in the broad sense of the word. However, we must
note that the word " concelebrate " or its Greek equivalent
συλλειτουργεῖν has never been applied to the people, but
only to ordained ministers, notably deacons, or to the
angelic hosts. [1]

PRIESTLY CONCELEBRATION

If the members of the Church take part in the celebration
of Christian worship " according to their differing rank

---

[1] B. Botte, " La concélébration dans l'Église ancienne, " *La Maison
Dieu* 35 (1953), pp. 16-17.

and office, " it is normal that priests participate as priests, that is, collegially as members of the presbyterium. This is true of the Mass, but also of other liturgical functions : in the Ordination of priests, the priests impose hands on those being ordained after the Bishop has done so as a sign of assent, " because of the common spirit and the likeness of their duty "; [2] when Baptism is conferred on a number of candidates, several priests may simultaneously administer the sacrament. So, also, in the East, it is customary for several priests to administer the Anointing of the Sick, in order to respect to the letter the counsel of St. James : " Is someone among you sick? Let him call the priests of the Church " (James 5 : 14). So too, in the West, twelve priests must concelebrate with the Bishop in the confection of the chrism and the blessing of the Holy Oils on Holy Thursday. Finally, one should not forget that community celebration of the Divine Office constitutes a true concelebration.

The participation of several priests at one liturgy, each performing one or another of the functions which pertain to his Order (homily, accepting of the gifts, breaking of the bread, distribution of the Body and Blood of Christ) or simply taking his place at the side of the president of the assembly : such is concelebration in the ancient sense of the word. It is still so conceived by the Eastern Churches which have not undergone the influence of the Latin West.

COLLEGIAL CONSECRATION

Though the priest is a member of the presbyterium, he is also one of the baptized who has personally received the power to consecrate bread and wine. Thus, for him, it is not only a question of participating in a liturgy

---

[2] *La Tradition apostolique de saint Hippolyte*, 8; ed. B. Botte (Münster 1963), p. 25. See also G. Dix, *The Treatise on the Apostolic Tradition of St. Hippolytus of Rome* (London, 1937).

which manifests the collegial character of his Order; he must also confect the sacrament, *conficere sacramentum,* within his collegial participation at the celebration. It was thus normal for theological reflection to center on the problem of the part taken by each priest at the consecration of bread and wine in the concelebration of the Eucharist. In fact, it was during these discussions of the twelfth century that the word " concelebration " appeared.

Rome had not awaited this date, however, to adopt in practice what seemed to be most certain : from the end of the eighth century, at least on certain days, we find concelebrants reciting the Canon with the Pope; [3] and Amalar was able to affirm around the year 823 : " It is the custom of the Roman Church that in the confecting of the Sacrifice of Christ the priests be present and that they accomplish it with the Pontiff by their words and their hands. " [4] Rome has kept to this practice since that time, as asserted a short time ago by Pope Pius XII in his statement that the concelebrants themselves must say over the bread and wine : " This is My Body; this is My Blood. " [5]

---

[3] Ordo III, 1; ed. M. Andrieu, *Les Ordines romani du haut moyen âge,* II (Louvain 1948), p. 131.

[4] *Liber officialis,* lib. 1, c. 12, 25; ed. I. M. Hanssens, *Amalarii episcopi opera liturgica omnia,* II (Vatican City 1948), p. 75.

[5] Pius XII, " Address to the members of the First International Congress on Pastoral Liturgy held at Assisi, " AAS 48 (1956), p. 718.

1. History
of eucharistic concelebration

1. CONCELEBRATION IN THE EARLY CHURCH

CONCELEBRATION IN THE THIRD CENTURY

The most ancient texts which explicitly refer to Eucharistic concelebration go back to the third century : the *Apostolic Tradition* of Hippolytus of Rome, and a Syrian document, the *Didascalia Apostolorum*.

The *Apostolic Tradition* describes the Eucharistic liturgy which immediately follows the consecration of a Bishop : " Let the deacons present the oblation to him, and let him, imposing his hands upon it with all the members of the presbyterium, give thanks saying : ' The Lord be with you. ' " [6] At other places in the same document, it is said that the priests perform the breaking of the bread with the deacons, [7] that they distribute the consecrated bread, [8] and administer the chalice, [9] for which they will be assisted by the deacons if there are not enough priests. The specific gesture which associates the priests with the thanksgiving pronounced by the Bishop consists thus in the imposition of their hands on the oblations. One can easily relate this gesture to the one which the members of the presbyterium perform at the consecration of priests. [10]

---

[6] B. Botte, *op. cit.*, 4, p. 11.

[7] *Ibid.*, 22, p. 61.

[8] *Ibid., loc. cit.*

[9] *Ibid.*, 21, p. 57.

[10] *Ibid.*, 7 & 8, pp. 21 and 25.

In the vivid description which the *Didascalia* gives
of the liturgical assembly, [11] we see the priests presiding
from the east side of the place of reunion, on either side
of the Bishop.   It is in regard to the reception which
the community must accord a visiting brother that the
matter of concelebration is discussed.   When the Bishop
of the place receives a foreign Bishop, he first asks the
visitor to give the homily, " because the advice and
corrections of strangers is very useful; " and then he
invites him to say the Eucharistic prayer : " When you
offer the gifts, he will speak. "   But if he declines the
invitation, he is to say at least the blessing of the wine :
" If he is modest, and wishes to leave this honor to you
rather than do the offering himself, he will in any case
speak over the cup. "   The two Bishops thus share the
consecration of the bread and wine.   This concelebration
of the Bishop of the place with a visitor helps us to
understand the fact reported by St. Irenaeus in the preceding century : when, in 154, Pope Anicetus received
St. Polycarp, the Bishop of Smyrna, in a visit to Rome,
" he deferred the Eucharist to him. " [12]   It is evident
that Anicetus was present at the Eucharist celebrated by
Polycarp and participated in it in the same manner as
the Bishop in the *Didascalia* when the latter invited his
visitor to pronounce the prayer of benediction.

CONCELEBRATIONS IN THE FOURTH
AND FIFTH CENTURIES

Allusions to concelebration are not lacking in the patristic
documents of the fourth and fifth centuries. [13]   We find

---

[11] *La Didascalia des douze apôtres,* c. 12; ed. F. Nau (Paris 1912),
pp. 111-115.   See also R. H. Connolly, *Didascalia apostolorum* (Oxford,
1929).   This description may be found in *La Maison Dieu* 60 (1959),
pp. 37-39.

[12] Eusebius, *Ecclesiastical History,* V, 24, 17.

[13] See Martène, *De antiquis Ecclesiae ritibus,* lib. 1, c. 3, art. 8, 2;
(Antwerp 1763), I, pp. 119-120.

St. Cyril of Jerusalem explaining to his neophytes why they have seen " the deacon giving to the celebrant and to the presbyters about the altar of God water to wash their hands. " [14]   Pseudo-Dionysius is even more precise : " It is necessary that those who will go on to the sacred action most pure be purified. " [15]

Canonical documents, heirs of the *Apostolic Tradition*, continue to mention the imposition of hands of the concelebrants over the oblation : " The Bishop will impose his hands over the bread placed on the altar, and the priests will impose their hands at the same time; others will limit themselves to participation, " declares the *Testamentum Domini*. [16]   The *Apostolic Constitutions* make no allusion to this act, but say : " The Bishop, having put on a magnificent vestment, begins to pray with the priests, and then goes to the altar where he makes the sign of the cross with his hand on his forehead, saying, ' May the grace of Almighty God... ' "   No intervention by the priests is indicated in the rest of the celebration, except that they are the first to receive Communion from the hands of the Bishop; it is the Bishop who gives Communion to each, with the assistance of the deacon who administers the chalice. [17]

At Rome, in the beginning of the fifth century, the concelebration of the Pope and his presbyterium seems to have been the normal manner of celebrating the Eucharist on days other than Sunday, and, already for

---

[14] Cyril of Jerusalem, *Catéchèses*, 23, 2; ed. Bouvet (Namur 1962), p. 476.

[15] Pseudo-Dionysius, *De ecclesiastica hierarchia*, III, 10.

[16] *The Testament of the Lord*, c. 23, 2; ed. F. Nau, *La version syriaque de l'Octateuque de Clement* (Paris 1913), p. 32.   See also ed. J. Cooper and J. A. Maclean (London, 1902).   The Canons of Hippolytus (can. 3) reproduce textually the mention of the Apostolic Tradition.

[17] The Apostolic Constitutions, VIII, 12, 4 and 14-15; ed. F. X. Funk, *Didascalia et Constitutiones apostolorum* (Paderborn 1905) I, pp. 497 and 518-519.

some time, the Pontiff proclaimed at the beginning of the Anamnesis : *Nos servi tui, sed et plebs tua sancta.* The Roman Canon of the Mass developed out of concelebration.

2.   CONCELEBRATION
IN THE EASTERN CHURCHES

The Eastern Churches concelebrate today in two different ways : some have preserved the form of concelebration of the Early Church; others have adopted during the course of recent centuries the form which prevailed in the West from the end of the eighth century. [18]

THE PRIMITIVE FORM OF CONCELEBRATION

The primitive form of concelebration is characterized essentially by the fact that only the principal celebrant recites the Anaphora, he alone pronouncing the words of Institution and the Epiclesis. How could it have been otherwise in a time when the celebrant improvised the Anaphora? It is to be recalled that the period of improvisation upon a given structure continued much longer in the East than in the West. In certain rites, it lasted until the nineteenth century.

In the West Syrian rite, concelebration was abandoned due to the lack of priests living in community. We must go back to the fourteenth century to find a description of the practice. At that time the Bishop presided for the Liturgy of the Word at the *bîma*, a large dais placed in the middle of the assembly with seats for the clergy and a lectern for the readings. Then the pontiff, encircled by priests and assisted by deacons, proceeded to the sanctuary, but it was not he who approached the altar :

---

[18] A. Raes, " La Concélébration eucharistique dans les rites orientaux, " *La Maison Dieu* 35 (1953), pp. 24-27. This paragraph is a résumé of his study.

the archdeacon designated one of the priests to celebrate the Eucharist. At the time of Communion, the Bishop gave himself Communion and then gave Communion to the celebrant and the other priests. This was done because in the eyes of the Church of Mesopotamia, the offering of the Eucharist pertained to the priest, whereas the Bishop ordained priests and governed the Church.

Even today, in the Coptic Church, concelebration may unite Bishops, higoumenes and priests around the patriarch. Yet it is a priest, called the celebrant, who recites the Anaphora; an assisting priest performs the incensing and recites the prayers of intercession (the diptychs). In Ethiopia, the Coptic practice is followed, the celebrant alone saying the Anaphora, unless several priests celebrate simultaneously at different altars.

Until the sixteenth century, it was the same in the Maronite rite : the concelebrants encircled the altar, on one side and the other of the principal celebrant, but without reciting the liturgical prayers with him. These latter prayers were said by a priest, even in the presence of a Bishop.

In the Greek Byzantine rite (except for the Melkites), the prayers and the liturgical actions are almost entirely reserved to the first celebrant. The concelebrants participate in the actions of the group, but they recite only the prayers of the Little Entrance, the Ektene and the Troparion of the Holy Spirit before the Epiclesis. Only the principal celebrant says the Anaphora. However, in contrast to the Churches of which we have just spoken, the Greek Byzantine rite has the Anaphora said by the Bishop or the first of the episcopal concelebrants, when one or several Bishops concelebrate with the priests.

WESTERN FORM OF CONCELEBRATION

Contrary to the practice of the Eastern Churches, the Greek Catholics of Rome and Central Italy adopted at the very latest at the beginning of the seventeenth century the type of concelebration which had prevailed in the Latin Church at the end of the eighth century : the priests concelebrated by pronouncing together the words of Consecration.   This practice became, in the eighteenth-nineteenth centuries, that of the various uniate Eastern Churches which conserved or adopted concelebration : the Synod of Mount Lebanon in 1736 for the Maronites and the Synod of Cairo of 1898 for the Catholic Copts; as for the Greek Catholics, Benedict XIV wished to oblige each of the concelebrants to recite all of the priestly prayers (1755), but, in fact, the ritual preserved a greater flexibility.

Concelebration of the Western type is not limited only to the Eastern Churches which are united with Rome. Under the influence of the Metropolitan of Kiev, Pierre Moghila (1596-1646), who was greatly influenced by Latin ways, the Russian Church has the words of Consecration pronounced " by all the concelebrants together, in a moderate voice, and at the same time as the Bishop " according to the rubrics of the Pontifical, which adds, " May all, as a single mouth, say the words together.... But to bless with the hand the bread and wine is the duty of the Bishop alone. "   The rule adopted by the Russians in the seventeenth century was accepted also by the Ruthenians.   As for the Melkites, they were directly influenced by the Latin rite through the young clergy whom they sent regularly to the Roman College of St. Athanasius.

Let us note, finally, a type of concelebration which is the manner of the West Syrians and of the Malankars, and occasionally of the Ethiopians : a synchronized Mass, with several priests celebrating together either at different altars or at one altar, but consecrating distinct Eucharistic elements. [19]

---

[19] A. G. Martimort, " Le rituel de la concélébration eucharistique, " *Ephemerides Liturgicae* 77 (1963), p. 148.

3. CONCELEBRATION IN THE ROMAN CHURCH

CONCELEBRATION FROM THE FIFTH
TO THE EIGHTH CENTURIES

Between the *Apostolic Tradition*, written at the beginning of the third century by the priest Hippolytus, and the short Ordo which describes concelebration on major feasts at the end of the eighth century, there is not a single Roman liturgical document which explicitly deals with concelebration. Nevertheless, the *Liber Pontificalis* and papal correspondence make numerous allusions to it.

In 416, in a letter to Bishop Decentius of Gubbio, Pope Innocent I declares that, on Sunday, the priests of the city of Rome who had pastoral responsibilities were unable to assemble with him to celebrate the Eucharist. Thus, on that day, he would send by acolytes a fragment of the consecrated Bread, the *fermentum*, to each of them so that they would not appear to be separated from his communion precisely on the Lord's Day. [20] Thus, in the eyes of the Pope, the customary form of Eucharistic celebration was one which united the priests around their Bishop to fulfil their ministry of prayer and sacrifice. Even more explicitly, at the end of the sixth century (597), St. Gregory the Great says in two letters that he invited the legates of the Patriarch of Constantinople to celebrate with him, in spite of a difference between the two Churches : *Mecum feci eos sacra Missarum solemnia celebrare.* [21] Three centuries later (879), after his quarrel with the Patriarch Photius, Pope John VIII, on the contrary, justified his own legates for having refused to concelebrate with the patriarch. [22]

---

[20] Innocent I, *Epistola* 25 *ad Dedentium*, PL 20, col. 556.

[21] Gregory the Great, *Registrum*, lib. 7, epist. 30 and 31; ed. Ewald Hartman, *Monumenta Germaniae historica...*, II, pp. 477 and 479.

[22] John VIII, *Epistola ad Photium*, PL 126, col. 871. Regarding this letter, see E. Amann, " L'époque carolingienne, " *Histoire de l'Eglise* (Paris : Bloud & Gay 1947), p. 492.

We thus see that the practice of concelebration was common at Rome during the high Middle Ages and was practiced among the Westerns and Eastern Christians together as well as among those only of the Latin rite. But in what did this concelebration consist?

First of all, it is certain that for the Popes whom we have just mentioned, it was question of a sacrificial act accomplished by each of the concelebrants. The idea would not have entered the mind of Innocent I that, in the carrying out of their *sacrificandi officium*, [23] the priests who were assisting him at the altar were officiating less fully than those who were at the same moment celebrating in the titular churches or cemeteries. In his letter to Photius, John VIII used the expression, *tecum... consecrare*, whereas at Constantinople the concelebrants did not pronounce the words of Consecration, and, at any rate, the Roman legates would not have been able to say the words because of their ignorance of Greek.

Until the end of the eighth century, the Roman Church did not know a form of concelebration different from that described by Hippolytus. For Pope Innocent, the essential aspect of concelebration was that the priests be assembled around their bishop : *nobis convenire*, and St. Gregory the Great insists for his part on the presence of priests of Constantinople at his side : *in celebratione Missarum mihi adesse debuerunt*.

The *Liber Pontificalis* gives some details on the development of the rites. It attributes to Pope Zepherinus " the practice of having glass patens held by ministers before the priests while the Bishop celebrates the Mass, *with the priests remaining standing before him.* " It continues : " Thus, the Mass is celebrated... The Consecration being completed, the priest receives from the hand of the Bishop the consecrated crown of bread so that he may

---

[23] Innocent I, *Epistola 2*, PL 20, col. 476.

give it to the people. [24] In another notice, the same chronicle attributes to Pope Hilary the acquisition of important liturgical vessels which must be added to the twenty-five patens of silver acquired by Pope Urban, namely : a large golden chalice (scyphus), twenty-five large silver chalices, twenty-five containers to receive the offering of wine, and fifty silver chalices for the Communion. [25] If the attribution of such a decree or purchase to a Pope of past centuries has no historical value, one can nevertheless retain the witness of the *Liber Pontificalis* that at the beginning of the sixth century the stational Mass always reunited all the clergy around the Pope, and that during the Canon the priests remained standing, facing the Pope from the other side of the altar. At the end of the Canon, the concelebrants went to receive the consecrated bread from the hands of the Pope, and then came to make the fraction in the large paten which a minister held before each one of them. They then distributed Communion to the people.

The classical description of the papal Mass which is supplied for us in Ordo I from the end of the seventh century, [26] knows no other form of celebration : the suburban Bishops and the priests preside in the apse, seated on either side of the Pontiff, until the Offertory. When the Pope ascends the altar, the Bishops place themselves behind him, whereas it seems that the priests remain in their original place. The Pontiff recites the Canon alone : *surgit pontifex solus in canone*. When the Pontiff returns to his throne for the breaking of the bread, the priests remain at their benches and the acolytes come to present the consecrated breads to them in linen sacks, so that they may break them before distributing them to the people. Thus, the breaking of the bread

---

[24] *Liber Pontificalis*, ed. L. Duchesne, I, p. 139.

[25] *Ibid.*, p. 244.

[26] Ordo I, 24, 86, 88, 102, 116; M. Andrieu, *op. cit.*, II, pp. 74-105.

no longer takes place in the patens as in the preceding century.

At the end of the eighth century, a new type of concelebration appeared on certain days. Characterized principally by the fact that all the concelebrants recited the Canon with the Pontiff, it was eventually to become the typical form of concelebration in the West. A description of it is found at the beginning of Ordo III. According to Andrieu, the document " is evidently of Roman origin. Possibly, it was not united at first with those fragments which are now joined to it. " [27] Here is the essential content :

On feast days, that is to say, Easter, Pentecost, St. Peter, and Christmas, the cardinal priests come together, each having a corporal in his hand. The archdeacon comes and gives to each of them three of the breads of the Offertory. When the Pontiff ascends the altar, they encircle the altar to the right and to the left and they say the Canon with him, *while holding the breads in their hands and not on the altar; the voice of the Pontiff dominates, but together they consecrate the Body and Blood of the Lord, whereas only the Pontiff makes the sign of the cross at the altar to the right and to the left.* [28]

One will note at once the decline in pastoral concern to which this Ordo witnesses in comparison with the practice at the beginning of the fifth century; for, far from trying to give solemnity to the concelebration of the stational Mass on Sundays and feast days, it was precisely on these days that Innocent I sent the titular priests to their churches for the service of the Christian people. Yet, above all, we should note a determination to express in a sensible manner the part which the priests take indi-

---

[27] *Ibid.*, p. 124.

[28] Ordo III, 1; M. Andrieu, *op. cit.*, II, p. 131.

vidually in the sacrificial act, for not only do they recite the Eucharistic prayer (very likely from the *Te Igitur*), but each one of them receives three breads into his own hands. Amalar will refer to this practice a half-century later, when he says that at Rome the priests make the sacrifice " by their words and their hands. "

By the middle of the twelfth century, the concelebrants of the papal Mass no longer hold the breads of the oblation in their hands, but the rite remains essentially the same : seven cardinals ascend the altar with the Pope, *each one having a book*, and the Pontiff recites with them the Canon, according to the description which Benedict, a Canon of St. Peter's, gives of the Mass on Christmas Day. [29] Fifty years later, the future Innocent III will again evoke the custom of having the cardinal priests encircle the Roman Pontiff at the Mass and celebrate with him, [30] but it will no longer appear in the later *Ordines* of the papal Chapel, for concelebration of the Mass on feast days will have disappeared with the stational liturgy.

Concelebration in the West was destined, however, to perpetuate itself in relation with other rites. Numerous churches of France, for example, long preserved it in the Mass for the consecration of the Holy Oils on Holy Thursday; it was maintained at Chartres until 1846 or 1847, and at Lyons until the *Ritus concelebrationis* took the place of the local practice on Holy Thursday, 1965. [31] But above all, from the end of the twelfth century, concelebration was introduced in the Mass at the consecration of a Bishop [32] and, in the following century, at the ordination of priests. [33]

---

[29] Benedict, *Liber Politicus*, 20; ed. Fabre-Duchesne, *Le Liber censuum de l'Église romaine*, II (Paris 1905), p. 146; see also PL 78, col. 1033.

[30] Innocent III, *De sacro altaris mysterio*, lib. 4, c. 25, PL 217, col. 874.

[31] A. G. Martimort, *art. cit.*, p. 152.

[32] M. Andrieu, *Le Pontifical romain au moyen âge*, I, " Le pontifical romain du 12e siècle, " (Vatican City 1938), p. 151.

[33] M. Andrieu, *Le Pontifical romain au moyen âge*, II, " Le pontifical de la Curie romaine au 13e siècle " (Vatican City 1940), p. 349.

There is no need to emphasize under what decadent form Eucharistic concelebration was codified by the Roman Pontifical, where the concelebrants not only had to recite all the prayers of the *Ordo Missae* together, from the beginning of the Offertory to the end of the Last Gospel, but where the newly ordained priests concelebrated while kneeling and were not permitted to receive Communion from the chalice. The decadence of the rites, however, left the principle intact and the Second Vatican Council verified its universal character : " Concelebration, whereby the unity of the priesthood is appropriately manifested, has remained in use to this day in the Church both in the East and in the West. " (C 57)

2. Concelebration at the second vatican council

1. THE PROBLEM OF CONCELEBRATION IN 1959

On January 25, 1959, when Pope John XXIII announced his intention to summon an Ecumenical Council, the problem of concelebration presented itself very sharply. The renewal of the theology of the Church, the first syntheses of the theology of the laity conceived as a royal and priestly people, the discovery of the liturgical assembly as a manifestation of the Mystery of the Church, and the multiplication of groups of priests joined in common work, had all served to place the Eucharistic Celebration's communal character in focus. It was becoming increasingly painful to priests to participate in a Mass with the faithful without being able to receive Communion because they had been obliged to celebrate individually. During study sessions or at retreats, it was a burden to be forced to separate, after the singing of Lauds in common, to go celebrate a silent Mass, often standing close to each other in a room containing more than twenty altars. Would not concelebration be a traditional answer from the Church to this desire for a communal celebration of the Eucharist? For some, " such a revolutionary idea " was born in the concentration camps. [1] In 1946, Dom Lambert Beauduin said that " one has the right to hope with filial confidence and respectful submission for a return to the ancient practice. " [2] But, before the supreme authority was able to make a decision in this area, it was necessary to look

---

[1] B. Loison, " La vie liturgique dans les camps de concentrations, " *La Maison Dieu* 5 (1946), p. 131.

[2] L. Beauduin, " La concélébration, " *La Maison Dieu* 6 (1946), p. 19.

for answers to the new needs of our times, all the while remaining within the limits of existant legislation.

IMPERFECT SOLUTIONS

At first, here and there, some priests celebrated what one had to call " synchronized Masses. " Many priests, each celebrating at a separate altar, would recite together the prayers of the Mass and perform the gestures simultaneously, guided by a principal celebrant. [3] Sometimes, this form of celebration was adopted to assure unity and dignity among numerous Masses said in a single chapel humming with the dialogue between various priests and their servers; but it served, too, to set off the splendor of a large assembly. Sometimes also, it was practiced because of a lack of servers, for thus several priests might say together *Dominus vobiscum* to a single server, and he, in turn, could respond to all of them, *Et cum spiritu tuo.* In fact, one quickly found himself at an impasse.

Yet another solution was the communal Mass. A single priest celebrated, and the others, often vested in alb and stole, encircled him, all gathered about the altar; all received Communion. This practice was justified by the liturgy of Holy Thursday, when private Mass has always been prohibited, and further by the fact that daily celebration of Mass is not required of a priest by law. The practice of a daily celebration by each priest is fairly recent; it seems, in fact, that Pope Pius IX was the first pope to say Mass every day. Let us add that, for some, the communal character of the Mass seemed so fundamental that a private Mass had no justification in their eyes.

Theologians did not fail to reflect on the practice of the communal Mass, which seemed to them to be closely related to ancient concelebration. They distinguished

---

[3] " A propos de la concélébration, " *La Maison Dieu* 6 (1946), p. 118.

between sacramental concelebration, as at a Mass of Ordination when all the concelebrants said the words of Consecration together, and ceremonial concelebration at which, except for the celebrant, the priests only attended and received Communion. It was asked if a baptized man who had received the priestly character could be considered a participant at the same level as another of the faithful. To the degree that the priest carries to the communal Mass a specifically priestly participation, might he not conclude to certain canonical consequences? In the absence of the specific definition of intention in Canon Law, could not each priest bring to the Mass an " intercession " of a specific quality and thus receive, if not the *stipendium*, then at least an *eleemosyna*? [4]

THE TEACHING OF POPE PIUS XII

Attentive to all these debates on the celebration of the Eucharist, Pope Pius XII did not fail to intervene with great clarity. He did so both at the doctrinal level and the level of discipline.

In 1947, in the encyclical *Mediator Dei*, he discarded the false notion of concelebration of some priests who refused to celebrate without an assembly of the faithful present : " They say that the Eucharistic Sacrifice is in the proper sense a concelebration, and that the priests must concelebrate with the people present, rather than offer the Sacrifice individually when the people are absent. " [5] Against those who " renounce Masses offered privately and without participants as being far from the ancient manner of celebration, " the Pope recalled that " everywhere and always, necessarily and by its nature, " the sacrifice " has a public and social character, because he who offers acts in the name of Christ and of Christians,

---

[4] F. Vandenbroucke, " La concélébration, acte liturgique communautaire, " *La Maison Dieu* 35 (1953), recalls these debates, pp. 48-50.
[5] AAS 39 (1947), p. 553.

of whom the Divine Redeemer is the Head, offering to God for the Holy Catholic Church. " [6]

Seven years later, in an address given to the Cardinals and Bishops on November 2, 1954, Pius XII returned to the question of the communal Mass and the private Mass in order to " establish the nature of the act which consists in hearing or in celebrating the Mass, " and he declared that " the assertion which is spread about today not only by laymen but even by certain theologians and priests, that a single Mass at which a hundred priests religiously participate is equal to a hundred Masses celebrated by a hundred priests, must be rejected as an erroneous opinion. " In fact, as assistants at the Mass, the priests " in no way represent Christ in the act of sacrifice but are to be compared to laymen attending the Mass. " [7]

Finally, in the discourse which he addressed to the members of the International Congress of Pastoral Liturgy at Assisi, on September 22, 1956, the Pope adopted the distinction between sacramental concelebration and ceremonial concelebration in order to affirm that in concelebration in the proper sense " it is not enough to have and to manifest the will to make one's own the words and actions of the celebrant. The concelebrants must themselves say over the bread and the wine, ' This is My Body, ' ' This is My Blood; ' or else their concelebration is pure ceremony. " And the Pope continued, saying that " the decisive question (for concelebration, as for the Mass of a priest alone) is not in knowing what fruit the soul takes from it, but what is the nature of the act which is done : Does the priest, as minister of Christ, fulfil the *actio Christi se ipsum sacrificantis et offerentis* or does he not? " [8] In order to draw attention to this position of the Sovereign Pontiff and to nullify further controversy, the

---

[6] *Ibid.*, p. 556.

[7] AAS 45 (1954), p. 669.

[8] AAS 48 (1956), p. 718.

Holy Office responded on May 23, 1957, to the question on the validity of a silent concelebration : " Only he who pronounces the words of Consecration celebrates validly. " [9]

Although firm on the conditions for validity of the Eucharistic celebration, Pope Pius XII was personally favorable to the extending of concelebration in the Latin Church. It was he who restored sacramental concelebration to the rite of episcopal consecration in 1944, by the apostolic constitution *Episcopalis consecrationis*. [10] Death came before he had made a decision on such a grave question. He had only been able to promulgate the Instruction *De musica sacra*, which codified his thought on the subject of communal Masses and on synchronized Masses : although he prohibited the latter (MS 39), he was not opposed to permitting priests " to assist at a single Mass at which they would receive Holy Communion from the hand of the celebrant, " provided " that it be done for a just and reasonable motive, " with the authorization of the Bishop, and that the act did not involve the error noted previously (MS 38).

In fact, the doctrinal precisions made by Pope Pius XII exerted a decisive influence on theological reflection about the celebration of the Eucharist and opened the way to the decisions of the Second Vatican Council concerning concelebration.

2. *THE COUNCIL'S CONSTITUTION*

1. *The Preparation of the Schema on the Liturgy*

The extending of the use of concelebration in the Latin Church was desired universally on the eve of the Council,

---

[9] AAS 49 (1957), p. 370.

[10] The Pope refers explicitly to this in his discourse to the members of the Assisi Congress, AAS 48 (1956), pp. 717-718.

" at least in the exceptional cases when numerous priests find themselves united around their Bishop. " [11]   For this reason, at the time of the meeting of the preparatory liturgical Commission (November 14, 1960), a subcommission was formed to study the question of " sacramental concelebration. "

THE WORK OF THE PREPARATORY COMMISSION

The subcommission was directed to make a dogmatic and historical study of the origin, nature, and extension of both sacramental and ceremonial concelebration; and then to see if it would be agreeable to admit concelebration into general use in the Latin Church; and finally, in the event of an affirmative answer, to determine the conditions of place, time, and person, and according to what rite.

The conditions for validity in concelebration having been fixed by Pius XII, all discussions at the historical and theological levels, as well as the distinction between sacramental and ceremonial concelebration, proved to be unnecessary.   A chart of the present discipline related to concelebration was quickly prepared [12] and the essential matter for discussion concerned the precise occasions for which it would be suitable to extend the use of concelebration in the West.

If many priests, especially among those living in community, wished to be allowed to concelebrate in order to escape the conditions under which they celebrated each day a private Mass, the liturgists quickly remarked that " concelebration is, in itself, a rare thing and rather

---

[11] A notice given by the French Episcopal Commission on Pastoral Questions and the Liturgy, " La pratique des messes dites ' communautaires, ' " *La Maison Dieu* 34 (1953), p. 147.

[12] The essential material can be found in *La Maison Dieu* 76 (1963), p. 90, note 1.

exceptional. " [13]   In any case, the pastoral point of view did not have difficulty in imposing itself on the work of the subcommission.

The fruits of this work found place in the two articles of the schema of the Constitution on the Liturgy which were approved by the preparatory Commission on January 13, 1962.   The occasions to which it was considered suitable to extend the practice of concelebration were approximately those listed in the text promulgated on December 4, 1963 (C 57); but, for the evening of Holy Thursday, preference was given to maintaining the Mass celebrated by one priest with the other priests receiving Holy Communion.   Certain ones held, in fact, that such a rite represented better the Lord's Supper.

THE SCHEMA SUBMITTED TO THE FATHERS

Before being submitted to the Fathers of the Council, the schema on the liturgy had to receive the approval of the Central Preparatory Commission.   This latter group, little aware of the depth of the liturgical renewal and of its biblical, theological and pastoral roots, judged severely the document presented to it.   In regard to concelebration, it retained only the possibility of the Mass of Chrism of Holy Thursday and at gatherings of priests " if one is otherwise unable to have individual celebrations and *de iudicio Ordinarii* " (March 26, 1962).

2.   *The Decision of the Council*

The debate on concelebration took place in the *aula* of the Council on October 30 and November 5, 1962 (at the 10th and 12th general meetings).   The majority of the Fathers who intervened judged the propositions presented to them as insufficient.   The religious would have liked

---

[13] A. G. Martimort, *art. cit.*, p. 167.

more frequent concelebration in monasteries and communities of priests. The Bishop of Lourdes spoke at the request of the French Episcopate, invoking two factors in favor of concelebration : one at the practical level—the difficulty of assuring the worthy celebration of individual Masses when they must be numerous; and the other at the spiritual level—the manifestation of the unity of the priesthood and of the unity of the sacrifice. [14]

Faced with such a clear expression of the will of the Fathers, the Liturgical Commission decided to take up again the propositions of the preparatory Commission and to add to them the concelebration of the evening Mass of Holy Thursday. It was decided also to suppress the restriction introduced by the Central Commission : *si ad singulares celebrationes aliter provideri non possit*, because " the reason for concelebration is not the impossibility of individual celebration, but the manifestation of the unity of the priesthood. " [15]

In its new redaction, [16] however, article 57 delayed the vote on Chapter II of the Constitution. The latter obtained only 1,417 *Placet*, on October 14, 1963, out of 2,242 votes, because there were, in addition to the 36 *non-placet*, 781 *placet iuxta modum*. The majority of the *modi* concerned the affirmation according to which " it pertains to the Ordinary to judge the opportuneness of concelebration. " Many Bishops felt that the judgment ought to rest with the Ordinary both for exempt religious as well as for diocesan priests. In order to respect the episcopal jurisdiction in matters of cult, all the while safeguarding the authority of the religious superiors over their own subjects, the Commission added that " it pertains to the Bishop to direct and to regulate concelebration in his diocese. "

---

[14] *La Documentation catholique* 59 (1962), col. 1520.

[15] *Schema Constitutionis de sacra Liturgia, Emendationes VI*, p. 22.

[16] See H. Schmidt, *La Constitution de la Sainte Liturgie*, ed. Lumen Vitae (Brussels 1966), pp. 105-107.

This precision only served to submit concelebration to general legislation (CIC 1261).

The preparatory Commission had given the main lines for the future Ordo for concelebration. The Conciliar Commission was content to say that " a new rite will be prepared for concelebration, which will be inserted into the Roman Pontifical and Missal. " (C 58)

Clarified by these final precisions, the two articles concerned with concelebration were solemnly approved and promulgated with the whole of the Constitution on the Liturgy. It was only fitting that the Council, which had made a gift of Eucharistic concelebration to the Latin Church, should enjoy the firstfruits of the new Ordo. The Mass concelebrated by Pope Paul VI and twenty-four Fathers at the opening of the Third Session (September 14, 1964) revealed to the world the value of concelebration as the sign of the unity of the priesthood.

3. The new ritual of concelebration

After Pope Paul VI had organized the Commission for the Implementation of the Constitution on the Sacred Liturgy of the Council (February 29, 1964), this Commission put at first place in its program the forming of a new ritual of concelebration. Among the groups of experts assigned to do technical studies, the sixteenth group received the duty of preparing the rites of concelebration and of Communion under both species. In this double objective, a prior decision had already been made : for concelebration was not even considered without the Communion of the Blood of the Lord by all the concelebrants.

1. The Forming of the Ritual

Father A. Bugnini, secretary of the Liturgical Commission, retraced the steps in the development of the ritual of concelebration in the *Osservatore Romano*, March 26, 1965 :

The first schema for a Ritus servandus in concelebratione missae romanae *dates from November, 1963, when it was prepared by one of the best experts on the subject. In March, 1964, the formation of the* Consilium *anticipated the nomination of a special study group for the rite of concelebration and of Communion under both species. The group went to work immediately, and by April 2, 1964, sent the first official schema prepared on fifteen large mimeographed pages, to about thirty consultors for examination. The numerous observations received were used to a large extent in the preparation of a second schema around which gathered, on May 21, the same group of experts coming from all parts of the world and chosen from all pertinent sectors of the Church.*
It was thus possible, on June 6, to send the " definitive " text to the members of the Consilium, *who were to discuss and approve it at their second plenary session, June 18 to 20, 1964.*

The text, corrected according to the observations made during this session or submitted by mail, was put into the hands of the Holy Father by the president of the Consilium, *Giacomo Cardinal Lercaro, during an audience on June 26, and the Pope permitted concelebrations to be performed* ad experimentum. [1]

The experimental phase continued for eight months. Six Benedictine Abbeys (San Anselmo at Rome, Montserrat in Spain, Encalcat in France, Maredsous in Belgium, Maria-Laach in Germany, and Collegeville in the United States) plus the Dominican convent of Saulchoir (near Paris), received authorization to concelebrate several times each month, on condition that the number of twenty concelebrants not be exceeded, and that a report be sent to the secretary of the Commission with, if possible, some photographs. Soon, indults were given to the Bishops and to certain episcopal conferences with the same conditions. " In all, " says Father Bugnini, " there were more than 1,500 concelebrations. "

It was at the end of this most fruitful period of experimentation, unique in the annals of the liturgy, that the decree *Ecclesiae semper* was promulgated, March 7, 1965, under the joint authority of the Consilium and the Congregation of Rites. The ritual of concelebration and that of Communion under both species became the law of the Latin rite beginning on Holy Thursday, April 15, 1965.

No day could have been better chosen for the installation of concelebration. It was with wonder and enthusiasm that the Christian People saw, that evening, its priests united about the altar, and heard them, for the first time, sing the words of Consecration.

2.   *The Guiding Principles of the New Ritual*

It was not possible for the rite of concelebration prescribed by the Pontifical for the consecration of a Bishop and the

---

[1] *La Documentation catholique* 62 (1965), col. 715.

ordination of priests to serve as the inspiration for the new ritual of concelebration. Though the newly consecrated Bishop concelebrated with his consecrator, standing at the side of the altar and receiving Communion from the chalice, he was obliged to recite all the prayers of the Mass, not only those of the Eucharistic Liturgy but also those of the Liturgy of the Word as well, which were said at a second altar specially prepared for this. As for the newly ordained priests, they remained kneeling behind the Bishop while concelebrating with him, reciting together in low voice even the formularies which the prelate sang, as, for example, the Preface and its introductory dialogue; and Communion from the chalice was denied them. The distressing character of this concelebration was underlined by the fact that the priests were vested in chasubles which they kept folded across their back until the end of the Mass.

Since the Roman Pontifical was of no help in the forming of the new ritual, it was necessary to look elsewhere for guiding principles. Obviously, one could look to the East; and profit was gained from the experience of the commentator on the schema who had concelebrated daily for several years according to the Greek Catholic rite. Particular importance was ascribed, however, to two precise directives : that of Pius XII and that of the Council. Pope Pius XII had said that, for a valid concelebration, it was necessary and it sufficed for all the concelebrants to say together the words of Consecration; and the Council had shown that concelebration is a manifestation of the unity of the priesthood.

THE PRAYERS SAID IN COMMON

Between the minimum required for validity at a concelebration and the maximum imposed up until this time by the Pontifical, what prayers should be imposed for common recitation by all the concelebrants?

The Roman practice from the eighth until the thirteenth century required the joint recitation of the Canon from the *Te igitur*. The norm seemed reasonable. But the Canon does not constitute a unified whole : not only does it mix prayers of intercession with the Eucharistic prayer, but it includes formulas which were not originally priestly prayers, namely, the diptychs *(Memento, Communicantes, Memento, Nobis quoque)*. In the *Canon Missae* of the Paduan Sacramentary (Roman Sacramentary from the middle of the seventh century), one reads after the *Supplices te rogamus : Si fuerint nomina defunctorum recitentur, dicente diacono : Memento etiam Domine.* [2]

In fact, it was decided to require the concelebrants to recite in common the central part of the Canon, from the *Hanc igitur* to the *Supplices te rogamus* inclusively, as well as the final doxology *Per ipsum*. Perhaps it would have been better to have had the *Hanc igitur* said only by the principal celebrant, since it varies on certain days.

Such a decision, breaking with a tradition of five centuries, had difficulty making its way in certain circles of the Congregation of Rites and at the College of Masters of Pontifical Ceremonies. It was thus that the booklet prepared for concelebration for the close of the Third Session of the Council (November 21, 1964) had the following note at the beginning of the Offertory : *Orationes dicuntur secreto sive a Summo Pontifice sive ab aliis concelebrantibus* (20), and, at the beginning of the Canon : *Partes, quae uni e concelebrantibus assignantur elata voce proferendae, ab aliis concelebrantibus secreto et iunctis manibus dicuntur* (29). The same applied to all the prayers of the Communion : *Omnes concelebrantes secreto dicunt* (48, 50, 51, 52, 53, 54).

---

[2] *Die älteste erreichbare Gestalt des Liber Sacramentorum anni circuli der römischen Kirche (Cod. Pad. D 47)*; ed. K. Mohlberg, (Münster im Westphalia 1927), n° 885.

THE MANIFESTATION OF THE UNITY
OF THE PRIESTHOOD

" The Bishop presides in the place of God and the presbyters in the place of the Council of the Apostles, and the
deacons...(are) entrusted with the service of Jesus
Christ. " [3] " Let that be considered a valid Eucharist
which is celebrated by the Bishop, or by one whom he
appoints. " [4] From the time of St. Ignatius, the unity
of the priesthood was manifested by the reunion of the
presbyterium around the Bishop or his representative.
Such a structure manifests two elements : the emphasis on
the importance of the function of presiding by the principal
celebrant, and the properly priestly participation of the
other concelebrants at the sacred action.

THE PRINCIPAL CELEBRANT

It is first of all necessary that the principal celebrant
appear clearly as president of the assembly. The hierarchical character of the liturgical assembly was eclipsed
when, at the Mass of Ordination, thirty voices said *Sursum
corda*. According to the new Ordo, only the principal
celebrant greets the assembly and carries on the dialogue
with it. Only he recites the prayers of the president and
gives the priestly admonitions. Only he blesses the
ministers, the assembly, the oblations, the incense. Only
he elevates the consecrated Bread and Wine at the words
of Institution and at the end of the Canon.

THE OTHER CONCELEBRANTS

Standing at either side of the principal celebrant, the
concelebrants must be clearly distinguished from the rest
of the clergy and bring their active participation to the
communal celebration.

---

[3] Ignatius of Antioch, *Magnesians*, VI, 1; ed. K. Lake, *The Apostolic
Fathers*, I (London 1959), p. 203.
[4] Ignatius of Antioch, *Smyrnaeans*, VIII, 1; ed. K. Lake, *op. cit.*, p. 261.

In order to manifest clearly to the eyes of the faithful that the concelebrants are truly celebrants, it has been prescribed that they be vested in chasuble. There were some who would have wished to see the concelebrants vested in stole over the alb or monastic habit, but this view was not generally favored. It should be noted, however, that apart from the principal celebrant, the concelebrants may always wear a white chasuble, except at a Mass for the Dead. The color is a secondary matter.

It is also in order to distinguish the concelebrants from other priests present that they are required to group themselves around the altar from the time of the Offertory; yet they are not required to stand immediately beside the altar (RC 4). It would be contrary to the spirit and to the letter of the Ordo of concelebration to envelope a consecrated altar with a wooden structure just so that all the concelebrants would be able to stand beside it.

The concelebrants complete all of their essential participation by reciting together the central part of the Canon and in receiving Communion in the Body and Blood of the Lord. Yet, one or another among them is called upon to say certain prayers (the diptychs) and to fulfil certain actions which are of themselves collective, as the breaking of the bread and its distribution.

One or another may also fulfil a function in the assembly, as, for example, if the president cannot preach the homily, it is suitable for a concelebrant to replace him in this function; and if there be no deacon, one of the concelebrants will read the Gospel, another present the chalice for Communion, and take the ablutions.

Such are the specific activities of the concelebrants. These are rooted in those common to the entire assembly. It is evident that all the concelebrants take part in the singing with the people, which culminates in the *Sanctus*: " The *Sanctus* is sung by all the concelebrants with the choir and the people (RC 35). "

THE UNITY OF THE SACRIFICE AND THE ACTION
OF THE WHOLE PEOPLE OF GOD

If concelebration manifests the unity of the priesthood,
as the Conciliar Constitution indicates, it equally makes
visible " in an incomparable way " the unity of the Sacrifice
of the Cross and the action of the whole people of God,
as the decree *Ecclesiae semper* adds.

The unity of the Sacrifice of the Cross appears in the
fact that several priests " consecrate and offer together
the unique Sacrifice by a single sacramental act, " according
to the decree's own terms. But it is further symbolized,
to the fullest degree possible, by the common chalice. In
synchronized Masses, each celebrant had before him his
own chalice and host. In a concelebrated Mass, the ideal
is to have " one host sufficiently large " and " a single
chalice of adequate size " (RC 17). In the past, the Roman
Church has always permitted a multiplicity of breads,
which were carried by the faithful in the Offertory procession and broken by the priests at the moment of the
fraction; but it remained attentive to the symbolism of the
one chalice placed on the altar, even if, at the time of
Communion, it was necessary to pour the consecrated
wine into several chalices of smaller dimensions for
administering. It was for this reason that Pope Gregory II,
when writing to St. Boniface, the Apostle of Germany,
in 726, said that " at Mass it is necessary to observe what
our Lord confided to His disciples. He took the chalice,
saying, ' This is the chalice of the New Testament in
My Blood; do this each time that you take it. ' It is
thus not fitting to place two or three chalices on the altar
when one celebrates Mass. " [5]

---

[5] Gregory II, *Epistola* 14 *ad Bonifacium*, PL 89, col. 524. See the
reproduction of the ivory diptych (Metz, c. 850 A.D.) in *Dictionnaire
d'archéologie chrétienne et liturgie*, III, col. 2476; see also a reproduction
in A. G. Martimort, *L'Église en prière*, 3rd ed. (Desclée & Cie 1965),
p. 320.

As for the participation of " the whole people of God arranged hierarchically and acting together, " it must be prepared by a careful instruction (RC 11) and aided by the way in which the celebrants are placed in the sanctuary : " Provision should be made so that the faithful may see the sacred rite well; accordingly, the concelebrants should not stand on the side of the altar which faces the people " (RC 4). Thus, the circle of concelebrants should not be closed around the altar, but should be opened out toward the people : *Nos servi tui, sed et plebs tua sancta.* The unity of the royal and priestly people around its priests and, on certain days, around its Bishop, is expressed with particular force in the united singing of the *Sanctus* and in the Lord's Prayer.

The first initiation of the faithful to concelebration can consist in a commentary on the decree *Ecclesiae semper*, where an excellent explanation shows how such a celebration of the Eucharist " truly realizes the principal manifestation of the unity of the Church in the unity of the Sacrifice and of the Priesthood, in a single thanksgiving which is performed at a single altar by the ministers and the holy people. " If, however, concelebration is to be practiced frequently in a church or chapel, it is indispensable to show the laity why " each of the concelebrants may legitimately receive a stipend, according to the law " (RC 10) for some may be shocked by such a practice.

3.   *The Singing of the Canon*

Numerous Christians from our Western countries who have had the occasion to participate in an Eastern Liturgy have been filled with admiration by the sacred character of the rite, the singing by the concelebrants of the words of Institution in Greek, Arabic or Slavonic. The Latin rite seems dull by comparison. This liturgical richness is now available to the faithful of the Latin rite thanks to the singing of the Canon by the concelebrants at the solemn Mass. The rite of concelebration has thus received an increase in beauty and evocative power. There is no doubt that the singing of the Consecration by all the concelebrants is what strikes the faithful at their first participation in a concelebrated Mass.

The two melodies, which may be used according to choice, were developed by a special group, *coetus* 14, which has charge over the chants of the Mass. This explains why the melodies were promulgated prior to the ritual of concelebration in the decree which approved the chants lacking in the Roman Missal (December 14, 1964). [6]

Although the Canon of the Mass was certainly sung at Rome until the eighth century, no vestige has remained of the melody to which it was sung. It was on the basis of the most ancient version of the *Te Deum* (solemn tone) that the new elaborate tone was formed. As for the other, it employs the tone of the collect for the prayers as a whole, and the psalm tone for the words of the Lord at the Institution. [7] It will be noted that both tones put in relief not only the words of Consecration, but also the double invitation of Christ : *Accipite et manducate*, *Accipite et bibite*, as well as the command for repetition : *Haec quotiescumque feceritis* . . . .

Finally, a rubric clarifies that the chant may be limited to the formulas *Qui pridie*, *Simili modo*, *Haec quotiescumque*, or even only to the words of Consecration. The lawmaker could not more clearly express his desire of seeing the Canon of the Mass frequently solemnized by the chant in concelebrations.

---

[6] *Cantus qui in Missali romano desiderantur iuxta Instructionem ad exsecutionem Constitutionis de sacra Liturgia recte ordinandam et iuxta ritum concelebrationis* (Vatican Polyglot 1965).

[7] J. Claire, " Deux mélodies pour le chant du Canon, " *La Revue grégorienne* 42 (1964), pp. 92 and 99.

4. Communion under both species

The ritual of concelebration contains a detailed description of the Communion of the celebrants under bread and wine. It was for this reason that the rite for the Communion of clergy and laity under both species was prepared at the same time as that for concelebration, and was promulgated by the same decree (March 7, 1965). Before presenting a commentary, it might be useful to give a history of the forms in which the faithful have received Communion throughout the centuries, and to recall how the Second Vatican Council was led to partially restore the ancient practice of the Latin Church.

1. ## HISTORY OF THE RITE OF COMMUNION

" Take and eat of this, all of you, for this is My Body "; " Take and drink of this, all of you, for this is the chalice of My Blood " : these are the words in which the Roman Canon reproduces the words which Christ pronounced at the Institution of the Eucharist. Although the Lord is present under each of the species, as theology came to teach at a later time, the Christians of the first centuries were profoundly aware of the importance of the bread and wine as signs of the meal of the New Covenant. They received Communion in the bread and from the chalice, ratifying with their double *Amen* the words which the priest and deacon addressed to them : " The Body of Christ, " " The Blood of Christ. "

1. ### Universal Practice until the Twelfth Century

During the first twelve centuries, Communion under both species was practiced as much in the West as in the East, not only at the celebration of the Mass, but even apart from Mass. It has been possible to assemble an impressive array of witnesses on Communion at the time of death under both species from Latin liturgical and hagiographical sources of the sixth to the twelfth centuries. [1] The ideal for the Christian was to die immediately after having received the Body and Blood of the Lord.

Although this practice was universal, there were nevertheless some exceptions. For a long time, as they left the Sunday Eucharist, the faithful carried the Consecrated Elements to their homes in order to give themselves Communion during the week. It is obvious that often they were able to carry away only the consecrated bread. On the contrary, the Eucharist was given in only one kind, the consecrated wine, to the sick who were unable to swallow the bread, and, as the Eastern rites still permit today, [2] to small children after their Baptism and Confirmation, in order to complete their Christian initiation.

In what form were the bread and wine presented to the communicants? One finds that various ways were employed particularly in regard to Communion of the Blood of the Lord.

THE RECEPTION OF THE BODY OF THE LORD

During the first millennium, leavened bread was used for the Eucharist. After it was broken, each fragment was large enough to retain its consistency when it was placed into the hand of the communicant by the priest. From Tertullian to St. John Damascene, Christian authors make frequent allusion to this sanctification of the hand of the

---

[1] M. Andrieu, *Immixtio et consecratio, la consécration par contact dans les documents liturgiques du moyen âge* (Paris 1924), pp. 114-152.

[2] E. Mercenier, *La prière des Églises de rite byzantin*, I (Chevetogne 1937), p. 351.

faithful by the Body of Christ. St. Cyril of Jerusalem gives a detailed description of the rite :

Approaching, therefore, come not with the palms of your hands extended, or your fingers spread out; but make of your left hand as if a throne for your right, which is about to receive the King. In the hollow of your hand, receive the Body of Christ, and answer Amen. *Then after you have carefully sanctified your eyes by contact with the Holy Body, partake of it, taking heed lest you lose any of it.* [3]

Men received the Body of Christ in the bare hand, but women covered the hand with a cloth called the *dominicale*. The Council of Autun, held between 561 and 605, requires that each woman, when she receives Communion, have her *dominicale*. [4]

From the tenth century the practice spread of placing the host in the mouth of the communicant. The Pontifical of Mainz from the middle of the tenth century is witness to this innovation : priests and deacons continued to receive the Eucharist in their hands, whereas the sub-deacons received it placed in the mouth : *ore accipiant corpus Christi*. [5] The substitution of unleavened bread for ordinary bread, and later the preparation of " small hosts, " certainly contributed to the change in the rite.

When the faithful approached the chancel, or even the altar in Gallican practice, in order to receive Communion, they evidently stood to receive the Body and Blood of Christ. The practice of standing to receive Communion was maintained long after the suppression of the Communion with the chalice, as various iconographic documents give witness. It is sufficient to recall the celebrated " Communion of the Knight " at the Cathedral of Reims.

---

[3] Cyril of Jerusalem, *Mystagogical Catechesis* 5, 21, ed. Bouvet, *op. cit.,* p. 485, can. 42.

[4] *Synodus dioecesana autissiodorensis*, can. 42; ed. C. de Clercq, *Concilia Galliae* (511-695), CCSL 148 A (Turnhout : 1963), p. 270.

[5] *Ordo X*, 59-60; ed. M. Andrieu, *Les Ordines romani...*, *op. cit.*, II, p. 361.

THE RECEPTION OF THE BLOOD OF CHRIST

Since the third century, the usual minister of the Blood of the Lord was the deacon, in the West as well as in the East. [6]   According to the *Apostolic Constitutions*, whereas the Bishop gives the bread to the communicant, it is the deacon who holds the chalice and administers it, saying : " The Blood of Christ, the cup of life. " [7]   The breviary has preserved in the Office of St. Lawrence a fragment of the passion of the Roman deacon, which witnesses to this practice.   It concerns a dialogue between Pope Sixtus II and his deacon in which critics recognize the hand of St. Ambrose : " Where are you going, father, without your son?   Where are you directing yourself, holy pontiff, without your deacon?   See whether you have chosen a worthy minister in him to whom you have confided the dispensation of the Blood of the Lord. " [8] The Roman Ordo from the end of the seventh century gives the same rule. [9]

COMMUNION FROM THE CHALICE

The deacon of the first centuries presented the chalice and the communicant drank directly from it with his lips. This is the most natural and the most noble way to drink. St. Cyril of Jerusalem describes it in these terms :

Then after having partaken of the Body of Christ, approach also to the cup of His Blood; not stretching forth your hands, but bowing and saying with worship and reverence Amen, be sanctified by partaking also of the Blood of Christ.   And while the moisture is still upon your lips, touching it with your hands,

---

[6] Cyprian, *De lapsis*, c. 25.

[7] The Apostolic Constitutions, VIII, c. 13, 15; ed. F. X. Funk, *op. cit.* I, p. 518.

[8] Office of Matins, 4th responsory.

[9] Ordo Romanus I, 114, 115; ed. M. Andrieu, *op. cit.*, p. 104.

sanctify both your eyes and brow and the other senses. Then wait for the prayer, and give thanks to God who has accounted you worthy of so great mysteries. [10]

The Church has always held to having one chalice upon the altar : " There is one cup, " writes St. Ignatius, " for union with the Blood of Christ. " [11] The most ancient chalices which we know, such as the admirable chalice of Antioch, now at the Cloisters in New York City, [12] are not of extraordinary size. Thus, it was necessary to use various means in order to give Communion to the large numbers of great assemblies. In some regions, the chalices for Communion of the faithful were filled with ordinary wine to which, at the time of Communion, was added some of the consecrated wine contained in the chalice of the altar : *refuso parum de calice in sciffo*, says the Roman Ordo. [13] This practice was also followed in Egypt and in Mesopotamia. " In other places, they held to the practice of a single chalice. Yet, as the amount of the Precious Blood lessened at the lips of the communicants, ordinary wine was added. This was the practice in Syrian lands from the seventh century, and, much later, in numerous monasteries of the West. " [14] Until the twelfth century, no one doubted the validity of consecration by contact; it was held that the contact of ordinary wine with the consecrated wine or even with a fragment of consecrated bread transformed the wine into the Blood of the Lord. Pope Innocent III (1198-1216) was the first to refuse such a concept of Eucharistic consecration. The scholastics echoed his teaching. [15]

---

[10] Cyril of Jerusalem, *Mystagogical Catechesis* 5, 22; ed. Bouvet, *op. cit.*, p. 486.
[11] Ignatius of Antioch, *Philadelphians* IV, 1; ed. K. Lake, *The Apostolic Fathers* (London 1959), I, p. 243.
[12] A reproduction can be found in DACL, VIII, cols. 847-848.
[13] Ordo Romanus I, III; ed. M. Andrieu, *op. cit.*, p. 103.
[14] M. Andrieu, *Immixtio et consecratio...*, *op. cit.*, p. 244.
[15] *Ibid.*, pp. 15-16.

THE USE OF A STRAW

One can receive Communion from the chalice by drinking from it directly with the lips. But out of respect for the Blood of Christ, and for fear of spilling, a straw has been rather frequently used. It was with a straw that the Roman deacon of the seventh century gave Communion to the people from the chalice. [16] This practice became widespread among canons and monks by the twelfth century. [17] At the end of the fourteenth century, the people were still receiving Communion in this manner at Masses celebrated by the Pope, [18] and it is well known that the use of the straw has continued to the present day at a papal Mass for the Communion of the Pontiff, the deacon and the subdeacon. [19]

The use of a spoon for receiving Communion from the chalice is much more recent than that of the straw, and has never known as extensive a use. We note it principally in Italy for the Communion of the new Bishop at his consecration. [20]

COMMUNION BY INTINCTION

In addition to Communion taken from the chalice or with the aid of an instrument, a new method of distributing the Eucharist appeared during the seventh century which consisted in giving the bread after it had been dipped

[16] Ordo Romanus I, III; ed. M. Andrieu, *op. cit.*, p. 103.

[17] Concerning the canons of the Lateran, see *Ordo Ecclesiae Lateranensis* of Canon Bernhard, ed. L. Fischer (Munich 1916), p. 58. Concerning the monks of Cluny, the Carthusians and the Cistercians, see J. Corblet, *Histoire du sacrement de l'eucharistie* (Paris 1886), II, p. 277.

[18] P. Amelio, *Liber de caeremoniis S. R. E.*, n° 85; ed. Mabillon, PL 78, col. 1332.

[19] *Sacrarum caeremoniarum S. R. E.*, lib. 2, c. 14, 13; ed. J. Catalani, (Rome 1751), II, p. 78.

[20] J. Corblet, *op. cit.*, II, p. 280.

into the wine. The first witness to this practice comes from the Council of Braga (675) which condemned *intinctae eucharistiae* in the name of the Gospel. [21] The practice spread, however, especially for Viaticum. It was during the eleventh century that it had its widest use in the West. Bishop John of Avranches († 1079) allowed it for the Communion of the people, *non auctoritate, sed summa necessitate timoris sanguinis Christi effusionis.* [22] The *Consuetudines* of Cluny say the same thing : " This practice is contrary to the use of other churches, but it is permitted for the sake of novices and other brothers who are less experienced, to whom it would be impossible to give the chalice without the fear of accidents. " [23]

The Roman Church has always shown a firm opposition to Communion by intinction since, as Bernold of Constance wrote, " This use is not authentic, for it is contrary to the institution of the Lord. " [24] Pascal II (1099-1118) uses the same language as the Abbot of Cluny, saying : " One must not be carried away by a human innovation from that which Christ Himself did and ordered to be done. Now Christ gave the bread and wine separately to His apostles. " [25] The argument is convincing. The Pope might have added that intinction does not obey the command of Jesus, " All of you drink of this, " for one cannot drink dipped bread, it must be eaten.

The progressive disappearance of Communion in the Blood of Christ led to the disappearance of intinction in the West, but the practice became widespread in the East, where several Churches know no other form of Communion for the people.

---

[21] *Concilium Bracarense tertium*, can. 1; ed. H. Bruns, *Canones apostolorum et conciliorum*, II, (Berlin 1839), p. 98.

[22] Jean d'Avranches, *Ordo Missae*, PL 78, col. 254.

[23] *Consuetudines cluniacenses*, lib. 2, c. 30.

[24] *Micrologus*, c. 19, *De vitanda intinctione*, PL 151, col. 989.

[25] Pascal II, *Epistola 85 ad Pontium Cluniacensem abbatem;* cited in M. Andrieu, *Immixtio et consecratio...*, *op. cit.*, p. 13.

2.   *The Disappearance of Communion in the Blood of Christ in the
West and the Progressive Evolution of the Practice*

The disappearance of the Communion of the faithful in
the Blood of Christ in the West came about little by little
between the beginning of the twelfth and the end of the
thirteenth century, without the intervention or any prohibi-
tion by a Pope or general council. It was the consequence
of the development of the external cult of the Eucharistic
Species and of a more precise formulation of theology
regarding it. In the first place, Christians were increasingly preoccupied with the danger of committing some
irreverence toward the Sacred Elements (—it was at this
time that the celebrant came to be required to keep the
thumb and index finger of each hand joined after the
Consecration); on the other hand, theologians insisted
on the total presence of Christ under each of the sacramental species. Since Christ was present in His wholeness
under the element of bread, why risk some irreverence
to the Eucharist by giving the chalice to the people?
This new concept, foreign to the notion of a sacramental
sign, began to spread in the second half of the thirteenth
century. [26] St. Thomas Aquinas witnesses to the evolution
of the discipline in an article in his *Summa theologica* where
he treats the question : Is it allowed to receive the Body
of Christ without receiving His Blood? He answers that,
from the point of view of sacrament, it is fitting to receive
both the Body and the Blood, *quia in utroque consisti-
perfectio sacramenti;* but from the point of view of the
communicant, great care must be taken to avoid profana-
tion of the Eucharist : *ideo provide in quibusdam ecclesii.*

---

[26] Sometimes, to place this abandon of the Communion of the faithful
from the chalice all the way back to the beginning of the 12th century
a passage from a poem by Rudolph of Saint-Trond consecrated to the
Eucharist is cited. But the authenticity of this text is not certain
and its meaning remains disputed. Mabillon saw here a condemnation
of intinction : Mabillon, *Annales Ordinis S. Benedicti*, VI (Paris 1739)
bk. 73, p. 14.

*observatur ut populo sanguis sumendus non detur, sed solum
a sacerdote sumatur.* [27]

The chalice was refused first to the laity, then to
Religious and Clerics in Minor Orders, and finally to the
deacon and subdeacon of the Mass. For the Cistercians,
the chalice was denied to the brothers and sisters in 1261,
but to the sacred ministers only in 1437. Nevertheless,
Communion under both species for the ministers persisted
for a long time in monasteries in other regions. It was
still practiced at Saint-Denis and at Cluny during the
eighteenth century. It is still prescribed for a papal
Mass where, until the end of the nineteenth century,
the Sovereign Pontiff was assisted by a true Cardinal-
deacon.

In many regions, once Communion in the Blood of
Christ was abolished for the faithful, ordinary wine took
the place of consecrated wine in the chalice presented
to the people. The chalice of Communion became the
chalice of purification. Its use is prescribed in the Ceremonial for Bishops at the general Communion of Easter
(CE, bk. 2, c. 29, 3) and by the Pontifical for the Communion of the newly ordained at the Mass of Ordination.
Often, one drew with a straw from the chalice of ablution.
Certain synods of the seventeenth century recommended
that priests warn uninstructed people not to confuse
the wine of the ablutions with the Precious Blood. It
was for this reason that the practice was suppressed in
Paris in 1670. [28]

THE LEGISLATION OF THE COUNCILS

The abandonment of Communion under both species,
begun by general practice, came to be sanctioned by two
Ecumenical Councils, the Council of Constance and
of Trent.

---

[27] St. Thomas Aquinas, *Summa theologica*, III, q. 80, art. 12.
[28] J. Corblet, *op. cit.*, I, p. 622.

THE COUNCIL OF CONSTANCE (1415)

By the beginning of the fifteenth century, there were few regions where the laity was still permitted to receive Communion from the chalice. [29] It was at this time that the Czech movement for reform, under the direction of the priest John Huss, tried to restore for the faithful Communion under both kinds. The initiative of the campaign for Communion *sub utraque (specie)* did not come from Huss himself, but from his friend Jakoubek, rector of the Church of St. Michael at Prague. The claim of those who came to be called " utraquists " was not based on a theological error in regard to the Eucharist. Rather, " in the perspective of the people of Prague at that time, the practice signified for many that one privilege among many was being taken away from the priest, thus lessening his superiority over the laity. At the same time, it indicated a recourse to the Gospel rather than to the Church for determining all the details of worship. " [30]

The question was submitted to the Council of Constance by the Bishop of Litomerice. On June 15, 1415, the Council issued a disciplinary decree which prohibited not only the Communion under both species for the faithful but also refused the wish of some for the suppression of the eucharistic fast. The decree may be summed up as follows : Although Christ instituted the Eucharist after He had eaten, and although He gave the Eucharist to His apostles under the species of bread and wine, the Church introduced the practice of fasting and the custom of giving Communion under one kind to all except the celebrant long ago and with good reason *(consuetudo rationabiliter introducta et diutissime observata)*. This custom, which was established to avoid danger and scandal and

---

[29] E. Delaruelle, *L'Église au temps du Grand Schisme et de la crise conci-liaire*, volume 14 of *Histoire de l'Église*, ed. Fliche-Martin (Paris 1964), p. 748.
[30] *Ibid.*, p. 1104.

is justified by the fact that one receives the whole Christ under each of the species, must be observed as law which may not be rejected nor modified without the authority of the Church. It is thus erroneous to say that the observance of this law is sacrilegious and illicit; and those who insist to the contrary must be held as heretics. As an appendix to this decree, the Council excommunicated priests who would give Communion under both species to the people. [31]

THE COUNCIL OF TRENT (1562)

The Council of Constance had reacted against an innovation taken outside legitimate authority. The Council of Trent had to deal with the same problem in a much more serious situation. In spite of profoundly different views concerning the nature of the Eucharist, the principal reformers, Luther, Zwingli, and Calvin were unanimous in demanding Communion from the chalice for the faithful because, according to their view, the fact of sharing the broken bread and of drinking from the cup of wine belonged to the essence of the Lord's Memorial. Luther had introduced Communion *sub utraque* in his *Formula Missae* of 1523 and in his *German Mass* of 1526. In England, although Henry VIII in 1539 was opposed to Communion from the chalice, Parliament made it law in 1557.

Numerous Catholic princes, such as the Emperor Ferdinand and the King of France, asked the Council to authorize Communion from the chalice in their domains for the sake of peace; they said that this concession would stop the spread of heresy.

---

[31] *Concilium Constantiense, sessio XIII*, in *Conciliorum oecumenicorum decreta*, published by *Centro di Documentazione, Istituto per le Scienze Religiose, Bologna* (Herder 1962), pp. 394f.

THE DECREE ON COMMUNION

In view of a claim so widely supported, the Council wished to begin by affirming the faith of the Church. This was the object of the decree on Communion under both species and that of children promulgated at the twenty-first Session (July 16, 1562). Three chapters of the decree are concerned with the problem of Communion *sub utraque*. The essential is as follows :

1.   The holy Council declares and teaches that no divine precept obliges the laity and non-celebrating clergy to receive Communion under both species, and that one cannot, without damage to the faith, doubt to the slightest degree that Communion under one or other of the species is sufficient for salvation.

2.   The Church, recognizing its authority in the administration of the Sacraments, has been led by just and serious reasons to approve the custom of Communion under one kind, and it has decreed that this custom is law which may not be rejected and which may not be modified at will without the authorization of the Church.

3.   One must confess that, even under one kind, one receives Christ in His wholeness and integrity and the Sacrament in truth, and that in consequence, in regard to the fruit of the Sacrament, no grace necessary for salvation is denied to those who receive under only one kind. [32]

In commenting on this decree, the *Catechism of the Council of Trent* (1566) declares that the Church refused to permit Communion under both species primarily to oppose the heresy of those who denied the total presence of Christ under each of the species, and it enumerates the " just and serious reasons " which led to such a change in practice : the danger of spilling the Blood of the Lord on the floor while giving from the chalice to a large

---

[32] *Concilium Tridentinum, sessio XXI, ibid.*, pp. 702f.

number of people; the difficulty of reserving the consecrated wine for Viaticum for the sick; the fact that some are upset by the taste or even the odor of wine; and finally, the high price of wine in certain regions. [33]

THE DECREE ON THE GRANTING OF THE CHALICE

Having taken a firm position on the doctrinal level, would the Council categorically set aside the request of the Catholic princes of Germany and refuse all concession at the pastoral level? The Fathers vigorously discussed the principle of granting the chalice and the conditions with which the concession would have to be harmonized (August 28 to September 6, 1562). They were unable to reach an agreement, and they published only a decree in which they submitted the matter to the wisdom of the Pope :

Wishing to provide for the salvation of those in whose favor this request is made, the Council has decided to submit the entire question, as does this decree, to our Holy Father the Pope, who, by his singular prudence, will act as he judges useful for the Christian nations and salutary for those who request Communion from the chalice. [34]

Pope Pius IV, anxious to make peace, accorded Communion under both species to Germany in 1564, and the German Bishops immediately promulgated a *Modus ministrandi communionem sub utraque specie*. [35] But from the time

---

[33] *Catechismus ex decreto concilii Tridentini ad parochos, Pars 2, De eucharistiae sacramento.*

[34] *Concilium Tridentium, sessio XXII,* ed. Herder, *op. cit.,* p. 717.

[35] This imperial decree *de legitima executione concessae communionis sub utraque specie* (June 14, 1564) forbade intinction : the Blood of our Lord Jesus Christ may not be received other than from the chalice *propter formam in Ecclesia perpetuo usitatam.* See J. Leplat, *Monumentorum ad historiam concilii Tridentini potissimum illustrandam spectantium amplissima collectio,* VI (Louvain 1786), pp. 324-330.

of Pius V, who was personally hostile to the granting of the chalice, the Apostolic See clearly showed its disfavor of the new practice, to which the Jesuits were equally opposed. The concession was revoked for Bavaria in 1571, for Austria in 1584, for Hungary in 1604, and for Bohemia in 1621. [36]

3. *Communion in the Eastern Churches*

Most of the Eastern Churches have remained faithful, in various ways, to Communion under both species. But it must be noted that they remain faithful as well to a tradition, already firmly implanted by the end of the fourth century of rare Communion of the people. St. John Chrysostom gives witness of this both for Antioch and Constantinople, as does St. Cyril of Alexandria for Egypt. In his commentary on the *Pater*, St. Ambrose says : " If this bread is our daily bread, why do you wait for a year to receive it, as is the custom of the Greeks in the East ? " [37] This fact is mentioned only as a means of helping to understand a number of ritual particularities of which we shall speak.

THE MATTER OF THE EUCHARIST

Except for the Armenians, both Gregorians and Catholics, and the Maronites and the Catholics of the Malabar rite, all Eastern Christians use leavened bread for the celebration of the Eucharist. The Byzantines usually consecrate five breads, in remembrance of the multiplication of the loaves by the Lord. In principle, the other rites consecrate

---

[36] On this question see G. Constant, *La concession à l'Allemagne de la communion sous les deux espèces. Étude sur les débuts de la réforme catholique en Allemagne (1548-1621)*, Bibliothèque des Écoles françaises de Rome et d'Athènes (Paris 1923).

[37] Ambrose of Milan, *De sacramentis*, V, 25; ed. B. Botte, *Sources chrétiennes* 25bis (Paris 1961), p. 133.

a single bread, which varies in size more or less according to the number of communicants anticipated. Where unleavened bread is used, small breads are used for the Communion of the faithful, as in the West.

As for the wine, red is preferred, at least for the Churches not united to Rome. This was formerly the custom in the West, and it is more or less certain that Christ used red wine cut with water at the Last Supper. The Gregorian Armenians are the only ones who consecrate unmixed wine, as they have done since at least the seventh century. [38]

THE MINISTER OF THE CHALICE

In the Churches in which the faithful receive Communion under both separately, it is always the deacon who administers the chalice.

THE MANNER OF GIVING COMMUNION

For the Communion of the deacon, the Byzantine rite has preserved the practice of placing the consecrated bread in the hand of the communicant. For all others in the East, the Eucharist is placed in the mouth as it is in the West. Yet the rites vary among themselves as to the manner of giving the sacred elements.

First, one must place to one side those Churches which have adopted the Latin practice of giving Communion to the faithful under the single species of bread : these include the Maronites, the Malabars, and the branches of the Armenians and West Syrians united to Rome.

In the Alexandrian rite (Copts and Ethiopians), the bread and wine are given separately to the communicants;

---

[38] On the matter of the Eucharist, see I. M. Hanssens, *Institutiones liturgicae de ritibus orientalibus* (Rome 1930), II, vol. I, pp. 125-127, 230-231, 250f. On the rite of Communion, see A. Raes, *Introductio in Liturgiam orientalem* (Rome 1947), pp. 103-107.

the same practice is followed among the West Syrians. Among the Copts, the deacon gives the wine by means of a spoon, and sometimes by intinction.

The Byzantines, the Syrians of Antioch, and the Malankars, as well as the Gregorian Armenians, give Communion by intinction : some dip each fragment of bread into the chalice before administration; others put all the fragments of bread into the chalice and then distribute the Eucharist by means of a spoon. This second form of Communion by intinction, which formerly was widespread, tends to give way to the first for hygienic reasons.

Let us note, finally, that in all of the Eastern Churches, the faithful receive Communion standing.

4. *Communion in the Anglican Church and the Reformed Churches*

The Anglican Church and the Churches of the Reformation have practiced Communion under both species since the sixteenth century. Anglicans and most Lutherans use unleavened bread and receive Communion kneeling, although the English *Prayer Book of* 1662 explicitly declares that " the sacramental bread and wine remain still in their very natural substances, and therefore may not be adored. " [39]

Members of the Reformed Churches receive Communion standing or seated at their places. When they receive Communion standing, the communicants either pass one by one before the Eucharistic table, or else arrange themselves in a semi-circle about it. In most of the Churches, the communicant takes the bread in his right hand — the

---

[39] W. Keeling, *Liturgiae britannicae, or the several editions of the Book of Common Prayer of the Church of England from its compilation to the last revision* (London 1851; text of the 1552 edition), p. 233. Translator's note : regarding the so-called ' Black Rubric, ' see G. Dix, *The Shape of the Liturgy*, (London 1945), p. 674.

bread is normally in the form of long wedges of soft bread which have been cut in advance, and from which the officiant breaks a fragment for each communicant. The latter then takes the cup in his own hands, and returns it to the officiant after he has drunk, or else he passes the cup directly to the next person. [40]

2. COMMUNION UNDER BOTH SPECIES AT THE SECOND VATICAN COUNCIL

One would not be able to say that on the eve of the Second Vatican Council, Communion under both species was as vigorously desired as was concelebration. Nevertheless, several Bishops and even one national episcopate as a whole had expressed their desire to the Preparatory Commission to see the restoration of the Communion for the faithful with the chalice in certain cases. This desire grew out of the renewal of sacramental theology, which had thrown a new light on the importance of the sacramental sign, and from a deepening of the ecumenical spirit. Another influence stemmed from the fact that, since the promulgation of the apostolic constitution *Tradita ab antiquis* by St. Pius X in 1912, Latin Catholics found themselves in a paradoxical position : they could receive Communion under both species as often as they wished, *pietatis causa*, on condition that it was done outside their own rite (CIC 866).

1. *The Preparatory Schema*

The wish formulated by the Bishops did not involve a general restoration of Communion from the chalice. It

---

[40] R. Paquier, *Traité de liturgique* (Delachaux & Niestlé : Neuchâtel-Paris 1954), pp. 176-180.

dealt with a specific number of instances, in which the possibility of Communion under both species might be offered to clergy, religious, and laymen.

The Preparatory Commission entered fully into this point of view, and adopted the following proposition :

" *With all danger to the faith being avoided, Communion under both species may be granted in specific and determined cases, according to the judgment of the Bishop, and this for clergy, religious and laity.* "

The advantages which would flow from this concession were put into focus by the Commission : it would manifest the unity between the Eastern and Western Rites, as well as the love of the Church for its separated brothers; it would encourage the devotion of the faithful toward the Precious Blood; and the faithful would come to a better understanding of the fact that the Eucharist represents the Sacrifice of the Cross and announces the eternal kingdom, where one will drink the new wine as the Lord has promised (Mark 14 : 25).

The Central Commission accepted the project, with the specification that the anticipated instances would be defined by the Holy See, and in giving as an example the Mass of Ordination.

2. *The Decision of the Council*

THE DEBATE

The Fathers debated on both the Communion under both species and concelebration at the same time. This took place on October 30 and November 5, 1962. Some did not see the value of the innovation proposed to them; others hesitated to reverse the decisions of the Council of Trent. The press office of the Council did not render a worthy service only to the press correspondents in publishing a documentary note on the rite of Communion *sub utraque*, its progressive disappearance in the West, and the sense of the decrees of the Council of Trent. [41]

In the exposé of the amendments retained after the debate, the recorder of the second chapter of the Constitution has carefully set down the arguments given by the Fathers at the general session both for and against the proposition. In its favor, the commandment of the Lord, the ancient tradition, the fullness of the sign, the ecumenical motive, and also the possibility of giving Viaticum under the species of wine to the sick unable to swallow a particle of the host, were invoked among other reasons. In opposition to the proposition, others offered the tradition of past centuries, the authority of the Councils of Constance and of Trent, the scandal to the faithful should they think that they were receiving the Lord differently under both species or under one, or that the Church accepts today what was condemned yesterday. Arguments of a material order were also invoked : the dangers in administration, hygienic reasons, the difficulty of obtaining wine in some regions. [42]

THE DEFINITIVE TEXT

After this instructive debate, the Commission prepared some important modifications to the text of the schema. First, in place of the expression, *sublato fidei periculo*, which might seem to criticize the Churches which have always practiced Communion under both kinds, it proposed instead : *Firmis principiis a Concilio Tridentino statutis*. Next, it lengthened the list of examples of instances in which the Apostolic See might grant Communion *sub utraque*. One was proposed for the clergy : the Mass of Ordination; one for religious : the Mass of Profession;

---

[41] Text in *La Documentation catholique* 59 (1962), cols. 1545f.
[42] *Emendationes* VI, pp. 19f.

and one for the laity : the Mass following the Baptism of neophytes. But the recorder of the amended text insisted on the exemplary character of the instances enumerated, and that the occasions were not to be limited to those listed as examples : *Enumeratio tamen non est absoluta, sed exempli causa posita.* [43]

In this new form, the article was adopted together with the whole of the chapter dealing with the Mystery of the Eucharist on November 20, 1963.

3.   *The Application of the Council's Decision*

The application of the Council's decision depended upon an act of the Holy See, which would promulgate the new rite and would determine the list of occasions in which it would be permitted to give Communion *sub utraque.* This act took the form of the decree *Ecclesiae semper,* promulgated on March 7, 1965. Before commenting on the decree, let us note three characteristics of the new Ordo.

THE CASES IN WHICH COMMUNION
SUB UTRAQUE IS GRANTED

Among the twelve categories of clergy and faithful enumerated by the *Ritus communionis*, there are two which merit special attention.

First of all, there is the occasion of a married couple at the Mass of their marriage or of their jubilee. If the majority of laymen are to have the possibility of receiving Communion from the chalice at a solemn moment of their lives, it is necessary that this Communion be tied to the

---

[43] *Ibid.*, p. 21. On the detail of the amendments, see H. Schmidt, *op. cit.*, pp. 104f.

Sacrament *par excellence* of the laity : marriage. Many of the Fathers had asked for it explicitly : 120 of them had expressed reserve at the vote on Article 55 of the Constitution on the Liturgy precisely because the Communion at the Mass of marriage was not listed among the occasions allowed. [44]

A second category must be underlined : that of conventual brothers " who assist at the concelebration in the houses of religious. " Here there is question of a group of the faithful who may be numerous and to whom Communion under both species may be given frequently. In an abbey which has fifty conventual brothers and where the priests concelebrate everyday, there would be a relatively large number of the faithful receiving Communion under both kinds. If the experience is favorable, from both the spiritual and ritual points of view, the practice may one day be extended, as a certain number of the Fathers wished, to those Masses attended by a small group of Christians who wish to receive Communion in the fulness of the sign of a meal.

THE FLEXIBILITY OF THE RITE

Those who conceived the new Ordo were careful to restore the most traditional forms of the rite of communion : that the communicants receive the Body and Blood of Christ standing and the Blood of Christ be presented to them by the deacon, when a deacon is present. On the other hand, they wished to introduce the greatest possible flexibility into the rite, in proposing all the forms of Communion in the Blood of the Lord which have existed throughout the course of history or which are still practiced in the East.

---

[44] *Schema Constitutionis de Sacra Liturgia, Modi II*, p. 19.

THE INTERVENTION OF THE BISHOP

Whereas Article 57 of the Constitution submitted the given faculty to the judgment of the Bishop, the *Ritus communionis* adds that " it belongs to the Bishop, in each case, to choose the rite which will be used among those which are described. "   It would not be possible to show greater respect for episcopal authority.

2

THE RITE TO BE OBSERVED
IN THE CONCELEBRATION OF MASS
AND THE RITE OF COMMUNION
UNDER BOTH SPECIES

Text and commentary

SACRED CONGREGATION OF RITES

Prot. n. U. 5/965

GENERAL DECREE PROMULGATING THE RITE OF CONCELEBRATION AND THE RITE OF COMMUNION UNDER BOTH SPECIES

In regulating and restoring the celebration of the sacred mysteries, the Church has always been vigilant that the rites which contain the inexhaustible riches of Christ communicate them to those who are well disposed and also manifest them in the best possible way, thus impregnating more easily the souls and life of the faithful who participate in them.

The Church applies herself to this task with particular zeal when there is a question of celebrating the Eucharist : she regulates it and organizes its different forms so that they may express the different aspects of the Eucharistic Sacrifice and inculcate them in the Christian faithful. In fact under all forms, no matter how simple, where one celebrates the Mass, there is realized all the gifts and all the properties which belong necessarily to the holy Sacrifice of the Mass, in virtue of its very nature. However, among these gifts and properties, the following are pointed out here for a particular reason.

In the first place, the unity of the Sacrifice of the Cross, for many Masses represent but the one Sacrifice of Christ. [1] If they realize the notion of sacrifice, it is because they are the memorial of the bloody immolation accomplished on the Cross, whose fruits are received by means of this unbloody immolation.

Secondly, the unity of the priesthood: since, though many priests celebrate the Mass, all are ministers of Christ who exercises through them His priesthood, and, for this end, makes each one of them, by the Sacrament of Orders, participant in His priesthood in a very special manner. It follows therefore that when each one of them offers the Sacrifice, all nevertheless do it in virtue of the same priesthood and act in taking the place of the High Priest, to whom it belongs either through one or through many to consecrate the Sacrament of His Body and His Blood. [2]

Finally, the action of all the people of God is very clearly shown: in fact, every Mass, being the celebration of this Sacrament by which the Church lives and grows continually [3] and in which the authentic nature of the Church is manifested principally [4] is, more than all the other liturgical actions, the act of all the holy people of God, hierarchically structured and acting.

Yet, this threefold aspect which belongs to every Mass, is rendered visible in an incomparable fashion in the rite where several priests concelebrate the same Mass.

For, in this manner of celebrating the Mass, many priests, in virtue of the same priesthood and in the person of the High Priest, act together with one mind and one

---

[1] See Council of Trent, session 22, ch. 1 (Denz. 1740/938).

[2] See St. Thomas Aquinas, *Summa theologica*, III, 82, a. 3, 2^m and 3^m.

[3] See Second Vatican Council, Constitution on the Church, art. 26.

[4] See Second Vatican Council, Constitution on the Sacred Liturgy, art. 2 and 41.

voice; together they consecrate and offer the one Sacrifice by a single sacramental act, in which they participate together.

This is why, in such a celebration of the Sacrifice, especially if the Bishop presides, and when at the same time the faithful participate in conscious fashion, actively and in community, we find realized truly the principal manifestation of the Church [5] in the oneness of the Sacrifice and of the Priesthood, in one unique act of thanks, accomplished by the ministers and the holy people around one altar.

Indeed, by the rite of concelebration, truths of great importance which concern the spiritual and pastoral life of priests and the Christian formation of the people are proposed and inculcated in a living fashion.

This is why, for these reasons much more than for others of a purely practical order, the concelebration of the Eucharistic mystery has existed in the Church since antiquity under different modes and forms; and after having evolved in different ways, it has remained in use in the East and in the West up to our times.

For the same reasons, experts in the liturgy have continued their research and have asked that the faculty of concelebrating Mass be extended, and that efforts be made for a more suitable restoration of this rite.

Finally, the Second Vatican Council, having carefully studied the matter, has extended the faculty of concelebrating to a greater number of instances and has decreed that a new rite of concelebration be elaborated and inserted in the Missal and the Roman Pontifical. [6] Accordingly, our Holy Father Pope Paul VI, after having approved and solemnly promulgated the Constitution of the Second

---

[5] *Ibid.*, art. 41.

[6] *Ibid.*, art. 57 and 58.

Vatican Council on the Sacred Liturgy, ordered the Commission for the Implementation of the Constitution on the Sacred Liturgy to prepare as soon as possible a rite to be observed in the concelebration of Mass. This rite, after having been submitted many times to the examination of the consultors and its members, was perfected and ratified unanimously by the Commission on June 19, 1964, which stated that, if the Holy Father should thus approve it, this rite be experimented in a practical way in various parts of the world and in different circumstances before definitive approbation.

This same Commission for the Implementation of the Constitution on the Sacred Liturgy, conforming to the will of the Council, drew up a rite of Communion under both species, in which both the occasions and forms were set down according to which clerics, religious, and laymen might receive the Eucharist under both species.

For several months, then, numerous experiments took place throughout the world with the best of results, both for the rite of concelebration and for the rite of Communion under both species, and reports on this matter were sent to the Secretary of the Commission; to these were added opinions and considerations whose help has permitted the refinement of the two rites. His Eminence Giacomo Cardinal Lercaro, president of this Commission, made the presentation to the Holy See.

The Holy Father, after having studied both rites with appropriate deliberation, aided by the above mentioned Commission and the Congregation of Rites, accorded to His Eminence Arcadius-Maria Cardinal Larraona, Prefect of the Sacred Congregation of Rites, his special approval in an audience on March 4, 1965, and confirmed by His own authority the two rites in their entirety and in their details. The Holy Father has ordered that these rites become public law and that they be observed by all beginning on Holy Thursday, April 15, 1965, and that they be transcribed with care into the Pontifical and Roman Missal.

All things to the contrary notwithstanding.

March 7, 1965

Giacomo Cardinal LERCARO

Archbishop of Bologna
President of the Commission
for the Implementation
of the Constitution on the
Sacred Liturgy

Arcadius-M. Cardinal LARRAONA

Prefect of the Sacred Congregation of Rites

Ferdinand Antonelli, O. F. M.

Secretary of the Sacred Congregation of Rites

Rite to be observed in the concelebration of mass

Faculty for Concelebration

1. Concelebration, whereby the unity of the priesthood is appropriately manifested, has remained in use to this day in the Church both in the East and in the West. For this reason, it has seemed good to the Commission to extend the faculty of concelebration to the following cases :

1° a) Holy Thursday, not only at the Mass of Chrism but also at the Evening Mass;

b) at Masses celebrated during Councils, Bishops' Conferences and Synods;

c) at the Mass of the Blessing of an Abbot;

2° Also with the permission of the Ordinary to whom it belongs to decide whether concelebration is opportune :

a) at Conventual Mass, and at the principal Mass in churches when the needs of the faithful do not require that all the priests available celebrate individually;

b) at Masses of any kind of priests' meetings, whether the priests be of the secular or the religious clergy.

Nevertheless, each priest shall always retain his right to celebrate Mass individually, though not at the same time in the same church as a concelebrated Mass, nor on Holy Thursday. (Const. *De Sacra Liturgia*, art. 57.)

Commentary

The first article of the Ritual of Concelebration reproduces textually Article 57 of the Conciliar Constitution *De Sacra Liturgia*. The document promulgated by the Liturgical Commission and the Congregation of Rites thus presents itself as a putting into effect of the will of the Fathers.

We note the concern of the Council : the first purpose of concelebration is not of the utilitarian order; it is to manifest the unity of the priesthood. Moreover, the Commission does not intend to innovate : concelebration has always remained in use in the Church both in the West as in the East. It is rather a question of extending the faculty of concelebration to a certain number of cases.

Former discipline was to be found in the Code of Canon Law : " It is not permitted for several priests to concelebrate except at the Mass of Ordination of priests and at the Mass of Consecration of Bishops in conformity with the Roman Pontifical (CIC 803). According to the new discipline the occasions when concelebration is foreseen can be arranged in three categories :

First, there are three occasions when *concelebration is obligatory* : the new Bishop at the Mass of his consecration, newly ordained priests at the Mass of their ordination and the new Abbot at the Mass of his blessing must concelebrate with the Bishop from whom they have received consecration or blessing. The Council has extended to the blessing of an Abbot the rule which the Pontifical already had formulated for episcopal consecration and priestly ordination.

Next, there are several occasions when the *faculty of concelebration is granted by general law* : these are the Mass of Chrism and the Evening Mass of Holy Thursday, as well as Masses celebrated in Councils, episcopal Conferences and Synods. Hence, on Holy Thursday, there is no need for permission of the Ordinary for concelebration, but it cannot be said that concelebration is obligatory; though the celebration of private Masses remains forbidden, priests may simply receive Communion at the principal Mass, as they did up to now. Likewise, in what concerns Councils, Bishops' Conferences and Synods, if concelebration is permitted and strongly counseled as a manifestation of the unity of the priesthood, it is not imposed. After September 14, 1964, the Second Vatican Council had many concelebrations, but concelebration did not take place every day.

The third series of occasions when the faculty of concelebration is foreseen derive *from the authority of the Ordinary.* Article 3 gives precision and clarifies the intervention of the Bishop of the place and that of the Ordinary of religious. The Council here formulates the law in distinguishing places and persons : in every church or chapel priests can concelebrate *at the principal Mass* (and not at the hour which is the most favorable for them), if the needs of the faithful do not require that they celebrate several Masses. Likewise, priests, both secular and religious, may concelebrate each time they gather together, whether this be for retreats, study sessions, pastoral gatherings, or even simply friendly gatherings.

Let us try to see clearly in what spirit the Council has extended the use of concelebration.

The Council submits concelebration to three reserves : first, the right of each priest to celebrate Mass individually; next, the needs of the faithful; and finally, the permission of the Ordinary. The desire to preserve for each priest the possibility of celebrating individually was manifested by many of the Fathers in the discussions on the conciliar schema and was considered at all stages of redaction. As for the necessity of taking into consideration the spiritual needs of the Christian people for celebrating several Masses, should the occasion arise, on the same day in the same church, it was already considered by St. Leo the Great : *Quoties basilicam, in qua agitur, praesentia novae plebis impleverit, toties sacrificium subsequens offeratur.* [7] When speaking of a basilica " filled by a new influx of people, " St. Leo is not inviting anyone to multiply Masses to the point of hindering a true gathering of the people around

---

[7] St. Leo the Great, *Epistola 9 ad Dioscorum Alexandrinum*, 2, PL 55, col. 627.

the altar, but rather that all be attentive to pastoral needs. So also, it is not to oblige priests to have recourse to higher authority that the Council submits concelebration to the authorization of the Ordinary, but to recall that " the Bishop must be considered the high priest of his flock " (C 41) and that " all legitimate celebration of the Eucharist is directed by the Bishop to whom has been confided the charge of presenting to the Divine Majesty the worship of the Christian religion and to regulate it according to the precepts of the Lord and according to the laws of the Church *for which he has, in his diocese, under his particular judgment, the final determinations.* " [8]

In France, Bishops have wished to establish a certain unity in their practical directives. Rather than having each prepare a particular ordinance, they have worked out a common ordinance for the dioceses of each apostolic region. In general, they authorize a large use of concelebration. Still, they do not allow it for Wedding Masses, nor for Funeral Masses for the laity. [9]

In formulating a precise discipline for concelebration, the Council did not wish to take away with one hand what it offered with the other. On the contrary, it made itself the promoter of the new rite : concelebration has entered into liturgical practice and into the vision of the mystery of the Church. The historians of the Second Vatican Council will not fail to point out two characteristics : on the one hand, the conciliar assembly intensively lived what it taught, and on the other hand, its thought was profoundly unified. This is certainly true in what concerns the liturgy. From the third Session and especially during the fourth, the Council lived out the liturgical Constitution which it had voted at the end of the second

---

[8] Constitution *Lumen Gentium* on the Church, art. 26.

[9] See, for example, *L'Ordonnance commune aux diocèses de la Région Apostolique de l'Ouest* (June 2, 1965), art. 5.

Session. Thus, six concelebrations presided over by the Pope marked the Sessions of 1964 and 1965, and many others united Bishops and priests around the altar of the conciliar *aula*. Likewise, the teaching of the Council gave an eminent place to the celebration of the mysteries both in its doctrinal constitutions and in its pastoral decrees. In the decree *Presbyterorum Ordinis* on the ministry and life of priests, the Council recalled that concelebration " manifests in excellent fashion " that " all priests in union with their Bishops participate in the one priesthood and the one ministry of Christ "; regarding the community which priests compose it added that " each member of the presbyterium has with the others particular bonds of apostolic charity, ministry and brotherhood : this is what the liturgy expresses from earliest times when it invites the priests present to impose hands with their Bishop on him who is ordained, and when she gathers them together, unanimous, in the concelebration of the Eucharist. " [10]

2. In order that the unity of the priesthood may be manifested in the best manner possible, concelebration is allowed only once a day in each church or chapel. However, where there is a large number of priests, the Ordinary or the Major Superior of whom there is question in the following number may allow concelebration several times the same day, but at different intervals.

Commentary

Concelebration has not been instituted for a practical purpose, but in a theological view. It is this which the present article wishes to recall.

The Church, the Eucharist and the Priesthood are mysteries of unity, and priestly concelebration is a sacred

---

[10] Decree *Presbyterorum Ordinis* on the ministry and life of priests, art. 7 and 8.

sign of the unity of the Church, of the Eucharist and of the Priesthood. In order that a priestly community can concelebrate with dignity and fruit, it is indispensible that it adopt this new rite in this view of faith. It is understandable that certain priests hesitate to concelebrate because they feel that their proper priestly community has not sufficiently realized its unity in Christ and that, perhaps it constitutes a counter-witness before men. However they might recall that the Eucharist is also creative of unity and that concelebration aids greatly in rooting this in charity at the same time that it manifests it. But a hesitation such as this does them honor, for it shows that they have perceived the essential of concelebration.

On the contrary, it would be to misunderstand the nature of concelebration to make use of it as a means it is not a practical solution to the difficulties posed by lack of altarboys in a church or chapel where numerous priests are going to say Mass each day; nor is it a new way to add solemnity to a feast. It might be good at this point to bring this to the attention of different religious houses or institutions where, with the best faith in the world the members might think it necessary to gather together the greatest number of concelebrants possible in order to enhance the splendor of a profession or the feast of the holy founder.

Because concelebration is a manifestation of the unity of the priesthood, it is not difficult to understand that it is not normally permitted more than once a day in each church and each chapel. If the great number of priests requires a repetition of concelebration, permission for this must be asked of the competent authority, and further the sign of unity must be safeguarded in that fact that many concelebrated Masses cannot follow each other without interruption : one could, for example, concelebrate in the morning, noon and evening. The new legislation concerning the Eucharistic fast gives great liberty for the hours of celebration or concelebration of Mass.

Direction of the Discipline of Concelebration

3. It belongs to the Bishop, according to law, to direct the discipline of concelebration in his diocese, even in the churches and semi-public oratories of exempt religious.

It belongs to each Ordinary as well as to the Major Superior of clerical non-exempt religious and of societies of clerics living in common but without vows, to judge whether concelebration is opportune and to grant permission for it in their churches and oratories, as well as to fix the number of those who may concelebrate according to the norm given in the following article, if, considering the circumstances, he thinks the dignity of the rite warrants it.

Commentary

To understand correctly this article we must keep in mind the distinction which the law makes between the Bishop and the Ordinary : in his diocese the Bishop is the Ordinary of the place, but the religious who reside there also depend on another Ordinary who is their Major Superior.

The first paragraph does no more than take up, in making it precise, the declaration of the liturgical Constitution : " It belongs to the Bishop to direct and to regulate concelebration in his diocese " (C 57 § 2), in application of the general law: " The Ordinaries of places must watch that the prescriptions of the sacred canons are observed with care " (CIC 1261 § 1). In a more pastoral style the decree *Christus Dominus* affirms : " Bishops are the organizers, promoters and guardians of all the liturgical life in the Church which is confided to them. " [11]

But, while it belongs to the Bishop to direct and to regulate concelebration in his diocese, this requires further " the permission of the Ordinary " in the broadest sense of the word, for it belongs to this latter to judge the opportuneness (C 57 § 1). Hence, in a church of religious,

---

[11] Decree *Christus Dominus* on the pastoral charge of Bishops in the Church, art. 15.

concelebration interests two authorities : that of the Bishop and that of the religious Ordinary. The Conventual Mass, for example, insofar as it is the central and principal part of the choral Office, must be submitted to the same authority as the latter. But insofar as it is an important act of public cult in the diocese, it must, conforming to canon 1261 likewise be submitted to the authority of the Bishop and take its place in the liturgical concern of the ensemble of the diocese. " [12]

The second paragraph takes up first of all the same terms as the Instruction *Inter Oecumenici* to extend the rights of the Ordinary " to the major superior of clerical non-exempt religious and societies of clerics living in common but without vows " (I 79), then it formulates the extent of these rights : it deals with the faculty of permitting concelebration and determining the number of concelebrants " if the dignity of the rite warrants it. " Evidently, the powers granted to the religious Ordinary cannot be exercised except within the limits of the regulation established by the Bishop. Thus, for example, where the Bishop limits to twenty the number of concelebrants for his diocese, the religious Ordinary could not change this number to thirty without having obtained the permission of the Bishop.

The Number of Concelebrants

4. The number of concelebrants, in each case, is to be determined by taking into account the church and the altar where the concelebration will take place, in such a way that the concelebrants can stand around the altar, even if not all can immediately touch the table of the altar.

Attention will be taken nevertheless that the sacred rite can be seen well by the faithful : accordingly, the concelebrants should not stand at the side of the altar which faces the people.

---

[12] P. M. Gy, " Commentaire de la Constitution sur la liturgie, " *La Maison Dieu* 77 (1964), p. 131.

Commentary

The concelebrants around the altar

Rather than determine a numerical limit to concelebrants, the legislator preferred that the number be established " in each case taking into account the church and the altar where the concelebration will take place. " He demands only " that the concelebrants can stand around the altar, even if not all can immediately touch the table of the altar. "

It is evident that all churches do not lend themselves to the same placement of concelebrants either because of their architecture or the size of the sanctuary. If the concelebrants are sufficiently numerous, some of them could be on either side of the principal celebrant at the altar, while the others form a semi-circle largely open on the side of the faithful, for care must be taken that " the sacred rite can be seen well by the faithful : accordingly, the concelebrants should not stand at the side of the altar which faces the people. " The opportuneness is not only of a practical order, but also of pastoral concern : in opening the circle toward the faithful, the concelebrants welcome the holy people into their sacred action.

From this point of view, the concelebrations which took place in the Council, such as we were able to follow them on television, did not constitute a model. The concelebrants surrounded the altar on all four sides; further, because the masters of ceremonies required that all concelebrants be able to touch the altar, the venerable papal altar was enveloped in an armature of wood on three sides in order to enlarge it. Here, we might mention that in some places, certain abbeys thought it necessary to install a new altar of greater dimensions in order to concelebrate there. It was never in the intention of the redactors of the Ritual of concelebration to suggest such initiatives.

The number of concelebrants

While the number of concelebrants is not determined
under the form of a *numerus clausus*, it is evident that the
problem merits reflection : " We cannot imagine the
indefinite multiplication of the number of concelebrants,
with the danger of rendering celebration impossible :
the theologian will worry about the recitation in common,
the master of ceremonies will be concerned with the
minimum required for dignity, the ensemble, the place,
the vestments, etc.   This is to say that concelebration is
not the sole answer to the problem of the presence of
thousands of priests at a Congress.   It is the practice
of Ordination which gives an indication of the maximum
number founded on experience : one should never surpass
sixty to eighty concelebrants in a sanctuary exceptionally
vast. "[13]   It is thus that, on January 6, 1966, Paul VI
concelebrated in the Vatican basilica with seventy-two
priests whom he had ordained.   But the concelebrations
of the Council gathered no more than some twenty-five
Bishops or priests around the Pope, this being the number
of cardinal-priests in earlier centuries.

The Ordinances of the Bishops of France demand in
general that the rector of the church " consider in each
case how many concelebrants can be admitted in relation
to the interior disposition of the church " and they determine the number of concelebrants which should not be
habitually surpassed : " the authorizations herein contained
are valid for concelebrations not going beyond twenty
priests.   In other cases recourse must be had to the
authorization of the Ordinary. "[14]

---

[13] A. G. Martimort, " Le rituel de la concélébration eucharistique, "
Ephemerides liturgicae 77 (1963), p. 168.

[14] *Ordonnance commune aux diocèses de l'Ouest*, art. 3.

Concelebration in Episcopal Consecration, Blessing of an Abbot and Priestly Ordination

5. In the consecration of a Bishop, it is entirely fitting that the co-consecrating Bishops concelebrate with the consecrating Bishop and the newly consecrated Bishop.

Likewise, at the blessing of an Abbot, it is fitting that assisting Abbots concelebrate Mass with the Bishop and the newly blessed Abbot.

At priestly ordination, all the newly ordained priests must concelebrate with the Bishop.

In all cases, the Bishop who is principal celebrant may allow still others to concelebrate Mass.

Commentary

Special note should be taken of the importance of the verbs which regulate each of the occasions of concelebration.

" All the newly ordained priests must *(tenentur)* concelebrate with the Bishop. " The same is to be said for the newly consecrated Bishop and the recently blessed Abbot : each of these must concelebrate with the Bishop who has conferred on him the episcopate or the abbatial blessing. The practice of concelebration at episcopal consecrations was already established at the end of the twelfth century [15] and it may be anterior. Concelebration at the Mass of ordination of priests is attested to since the thirteenth century [16] but it was not universal in the West until the fifteenth century. As for the Mass which follows the blessing of an Abbot, it had as part, from the fifteenth century, a pseudo-rite of concelebration in which the newly blessed Abbot said all the prayers of the Ordinary

---

[15] M. Andrieu, *Le pontifical romain au moyen âge*, I, " Le pontifical romain du 12e siècle, " (Vatican City 1938), p. 151.

[16] M. Andrieu, *op. cit.*, II, " Le pontifical de la Curie romaine au 13e siècle " (Vatican City 1940), p. 349; and *op. cit.*, III, " Le pontifical de Guillaume Durand " (Vatican City 1940), pp. 370f.

but did not pronounce the words of Consecration :
*Medius inter assistentes suos genuflexus, legit totam Missam,
exceptis verbis consecrationis, quae non proferet,* as we still
find in the rubric of the Roman Pontifical of 1962. It was
the Council which substituted for this hybrid rite an
authentic concelebration.

" It is entirely fitting *(valde convenit)* that the co-consecrating Bishops concelebrate with the consecrating
Bishop and the newly consecrated Bishop. " Concelebrants
to the consecrating Bishop for conferring the Sacrament
of the episcopate, as Pope Pius XII expressed it in the
apostolic constitution *Episcopalis consecratio,* [17] they must
have a serious reason for abstaining from concelebrating
with him the Eucharist.

" It is good *(expedit)* that the assisting Abbots concelebrate with the Bishop and the Abbot who has been
blessed. " There is a great difference between the two
co-consecrating Bishops of a consecration and the two
assisting Abbots of an abbatial blessing : the first confer
the Sacrament of Orders, the second accompany the
priest who receives a sacramental. But it is good that
the brotherhood of the three Abbots and their communion
with the Bishop be manifested and deepened in the
common celebration of the Eucharist.

" In all those cases, the Bishop who is principal celebrant
may *(potest)* allow still others to concelebrate Mass. "
It is even desirable that he do so. Consecration and
ordination introduce the candidate into the college of
Bishops or into the presbyterium; and nothing manifests
better this entrance into an *Ordo* than the concelebration
of all the Bishops present in the first case and representative
members of the priestly community in the second. The
same is true for the abbatial blessing : the concelebration
of all of the priests of the abbey or of a certain number

---

[17] AAS 37 (1945), pp. 131f.

of them with their Abbot expresses in a visible manner the paternal function which the new Abbot now receives at the center of the monastic family.

The Rite to be Observed in Concelebration

6. The norms which follow must be observed each time Mass is concelebrated according to the Roman rite; and they are to be applied, according to the rules of law, as well to other Latin rites.

Commentary

This rule is recalled in each of the documents which have regulated for ten years the liturgical reform : Decree of Simplification of the Rubrics of 1955, Code of Rubrics of 1960, Instruction *Inter Oecumenici* of 1964 (I 9).

7. Any priest of the Latin rite may concelebrate with other priests of the Latin rite, even if the Mass is celebrated in a rite other than his own.

Commentary

The Code of Rubrics had already allowed a cleric or religious to participate in the concelebration of the Divine Office, that is, its celebration in choir or in common, in a rite other than that to which he belonged (CR 157). The authorization is extended here to the concelebration of the Eucharist.   There is no problem of adaptation for the Latin rites which are no more than simple branches of the Roman rite, such as the Dominican, Carthusian or Lyonnese rites, for they all have the identical text for the Canon.   A choice is called for in concelebration between priests of the Roman rite and priests of the Ambrosian rite, for the Ambrosian Canon presents several variants in relation to the Roman Canon.

The present document does not authorize concelebration between Latin rite priests and Oriental priests. This concelebration did, however, exist in past times, as we have shown in citing the witness of St. Gregory the Great and that of Pope John VIII (cf. above, pp. 19 f.). St. Pius X referred to this practice in the apostolic constitution *Tradita ab antiquis*, which re-established the possibility of inter-ritual Eucharistic Communion : *Episcopi, presbyteri ac diaconi latini cum graecis hic Romae, graeci cum latinis in Oriente divina concelebrabant mysteria.* [18] Before promulgating the rite of concelebration, Pope Paul VI concelebrated with the Melkite, Coptic and Maronite patriarchs at the time of the Consistory of February 25, 1965, when he introduced them into the College of Cardinals and since then, several times, the Pope has invited the oriental hierarchy to concelebrate with him. One can hope that such a practice will not remain the privilege of the papal chapel. All the technical problems of inter-ritual concelebration in the largest sense of the word can easily be resolved.

Concelebrants are not to be Admitted once the Mass has Begun

8. No one, for whatever reason, may be admitted to concelebrate once Mass has begun.

Commentary

This rule is not only to prevent possible abuses; it flows from the very nature of concelebration. It is an action in common and hierarchically organized, in which each priest exercises a determined function which has been assigned to him by the principal celebrant before the procession leaves the sacristy : one will proclaim the Gospel in the absence of a deacon, another will announce the

---

[18] AAS 4 (1912), p. 610.

intentions of the Prayer of the Faithful; they will divide the reading of the diptychs in the Canon, others will take part in the breaking of the bread; still others will distribute Communion. In the seventh century, at Rome, before the Bishop gave the signal for the departure of the Entrance Procession, a subdeacon asked for the names of the chanters and announced to the Pope : " This subdeacon will read the Apostle and that member of the Schola will chant the Psalm. " [19] The *Ordo* adds : " After this, it is no longer allowed to change the reader or the chanter. If this should happen, he who would have made the announcement will be excommunicated by the Pontiff. " Without coming to such measures, it was indispensible that the present Ritual give a very firm rule.

Masses to be Celebrated or Concelebrated on the Same Day

9. a) On Holy Thursday, anyone who celebrated or concelebrated the Mass of Chrism may likewise celebrate or concelebrate the Evening Mass.

b) In the Easter Vigil, whoever celebrates or concelebrates Mass may also celebrate or concelebrate the second Mass of Easter.

c) At Christmas, all priests may concelebrate the three Masses as long as these Masses are celebrated at the proper times.

d) Whoever concelebrates with the Bishop or with his delegate at a Synod, in the Pastoral Visit or in the meetings of priests, may celebrate a second Mass for the sake of the faithful, if the same Bishop judges it useful.

In other cases, whoever concelebrates cannot celebrate a second Mass on the same day.

Commentary

Concerning the possibility of repeating Mass the same day, the Ritual assimilates, as it should, concelebration to

---

[19] Ordo Romanus I, 37-39, in M. Andrieu, *Les Ordines romani du haut moyen âge* (Louvain 1948), II, pp. 79f.

celebration by one priest and refers to general law, while adding an innovation and several nuances which we should point out.

According to Canon Law, a priest may not offer the Eucharistic Sacrifice more than once a day, except on Christmas and the Commemoration of the Dead, when he can do so three times, or with the authorization of bination which the Ordinary can grant on certain days for the good of the faithful (CIC 806). Since the restoration of Holy Week, we must add two other exceptions to the general law: on Holy Thursday, the Bishop who has celebrated the Mass of Chrism may also offer the Evening Mass; also, the priest who has celebrated the Mass of the Easter Vigil may also offer the Mass of the Sunday of the Resurrection. [20]

Basing itself on existing legislation, the Ritual of concelebration recalls that " he who concelebrates cannot celebrate a second Mass the same day; " but it grants to all concelebrants of the Mass of Chrism on Holy Thursday the right to celebrate or concelebrate again in the evening; it recognizes the same faculty for the celebrant or the concelebrants of the Easter Vigil.

For the three Masses of Christmas, the Ritual authorizes priests to concelebrate three times, but on condition that each of the Masses be said " at its proper time. " Hence, one cannot concelebrate the three Masses one after the other. This is indeed a very fortunate limitation. It is to be hoped that someday this same ruling will be extended from concelebration to the celebration of the Masses of Christmas and of November 2.

To be noted is the silence of the Ritual on the subject of the three Masses for the Commemoration of the Dead. It seems that one can apply to them the law formulated

---

[20] Roman Missal, Mass of the Chrism on Holy Thursday, 18; Mass of the Paschal Vigil, 12.

for Christmas : that one may concelebrate the three Masses, as long as they do not follow immediately one upon the other.

Canon Law grants to Bishops the faculty of authorizing bination on certain days when the good of the faithful requires it. Normally there would be no question of extending this favor to concelebration, for one priest is sufficient to satisfy the needs of a pastoral order. However, the Ritual allows bination in concelebration in a precise case : " whoever concelebrates with the Bishop or with his delegate at a Synod, in the Pastoral Visit or in meetings of priests, may in the judgment of the same Bishop, celebrate a second Mass for the benefit of the faithful. " The exception is important because it permits a better understanding of the essential reason for concelebration. Since it has as its purpose to manifest the unity of the priesthood, it is fitting that such a Mass gather around the Bishop or his delegate all the priests who take part in the priests' gathering. If one or the other would have to abstain from taking part in the common Eucharist because of the ministry, something would be lacking to the fulness of the sign. On the other hand, however, the pastor is bound to see to the needs of his proper community : he may have to offer Mass on the occasion of a marriage or a funeral or simply celebrate the Eucharist for the faithful who participate each day at Mass. It is for this reason that the legislator has allowed in such a circumstance a double celebration.

The Stipend

10. Each of the concelebrants may legitimately receive a stipend, according to the law.

Commentary

Though true that Eucharistic concelebration was practiced in the West at other times besides episcopal consecration and the ordination of priests, canonists were scarcely interested in the problem of stipends for the Masses of concelebrants. The Code of 1917 makes no allusion to it and the French Dictionary of Canon Law (1935-1965) does not even give one line to it.

Maurice de la Taille is perhaps the only Latin theologian to pose the question. In his treatise on the Eucharist *Mysterium Fidei*, he based himself on Eastern practice to grant to each concelebrant the right to receive a personal stipend, the purpose of the offering of the faithful being to see to the material needs of the priest. [21]

When we speak of Easter practice, we must not give to the expression too vast an extension. In fact, it was especially the Maronites who concerned themselves with the stipends of concelebrants and who legislated on the subject. Since 1579, in a project of a council which was to be held at Qannoubin but was not able to come together because of a plague, it was said : " Priests must fulfil their obligation of celebrating the Mass for the living and the dead; simple assistance at the Mass of another priest is not sufficient for satisfying an intention for a Mass : there would have to be a true concelebration. " The same prescription was formulated under a positive form by the Synod of Mount Lebanon in 1736 : " We declare that those who concelebrate in conformity with the rules satisfy the obligation of celebrating for the living and the dead and for the offerings which they receive for this intention. "

These acts of the Synod of Mount Lebanon were submitted by Benedict XIV to a study by a particular commission, which imposed some fifteen modifications in details in the texts of the canons, before the Pope confirmed them by the brief *Singularis Romanorum* of September 1,

---

[21] M. de la Taille, *Mysterium fidei*, elucidatio 28, appendix D, *De concelebrantium sacerdotum stipendiis* (Paris 1921), pp. 354-356.

1741. [22] Thus, they engage the authority of the Apostolic See.

Catechetical Preparation

11. Pastors shall see to it that the faithful who assist at concelebration be appropriately instructed beforehand regarding the rite itself and its meaning.

Commentary

A concern for preparing the faithful for all innovations in the rites, assuring for them an adapted instruction, never ceased to be present to the liturgical legislator ever since the restoration of the Easter Vigil. The Instruction *Inter Oecumenici* formulated the law : when the competent authority has promulgated the decrees of reform, it will always foresee a reasonable delay in application " so that, in the interval, the faithful may be informed and initiated regarding the rites " (I 10).

In what concerns concelebration, the instruction of the faithful could well be inspired by the decree *Ecclesiae semper* by which the new rite was promulgated (text, p. 71). A commentary can be found above (pp. 39-42).

General Norms

12. All the concelebrants must wear the liturgical vestments they are bound to wear when they celebrate Mass individually. Concelebrating Bishops, however, wear only the amice, alb, cincture, pectoral cross, stole, chasuble, maniple and miter.

---

[22] C. de Clercq, " Conciles des Orientaux catholiques, " *Histoire des Conciles* (Paris 1949), II : the project of the Council of Qannoubin, p. 9; synod of Mount-Lebanon, p. 246; Roman approbation, p. 272. The Latin text of the synod of Mount-Lebanon can be found in the article of A. G. Martimort, *art. cit.*, p. 149.

All the liturgical vestments will be of the color which is proper to the Mass. However, the proper color being kept by the principal celebrant, the concelebrants may in case of necessity use white, except for Masses for the Dead.

In particular cases, the matter is to be submitted to the Apostolic See.

Commentary

The liturgical vestments

Some may find burdensome the regulation that all the priests must be vested in chasuble for concelebration. They might wish a more simple type of concelebration for which it would be sufficient to wear alb and stole. The legislator preferred to conform to tradition : the obligation to wear all the liturgical vestments of the Mass for concelebrating is universal in the East.   The synods of the united oriental Church make mention of it in their legislation : the Synod of Mount Lebanon in 1736 made it a condition for validity for the Maronites, and the Synod of Cairo in 1898 imposed it *sub gravi* for the Copts. [23]   But there is also a pastoral reason for this obligation : it must not appear to the eyes of the faithful that the principal celebrant differs too much from the other celebrants, for all the priests must appear equal in the celebration; it is fitting also that one distinguish from the first glance the concelebrating priests from the ministers who surround them.

The present article nevertheless contains some mitigation of the law in secondary points.

First of all, concelebrating Bishops do not wear the liturgical sandals and stockings, nor the tunic and dalmatic under the chasuble.

---

[23] Texts are cited in the article of A. G. Martimort, *art. cit.*, *loc. cit.*

Further, if it is difficult to find for all the concelebrants sacred vestments of the color of the day, they may use white, except in Masses for the Dead, while the principal celebrant alone must be clothed in the chasuble of the color of the day. This permission is used considerably. Without it, concelebration would not have been able to spread as rapidly as it did, for it would have been impossible for parishes and religious houses to procure a liturgical wardrobe containing ten to twenty chasubles of each of the liturgical colors. Some day, perhaps, the legislation will be more liberal allowing, as in the East, diversity in the choice of colors. We know that these were not fixed until the thirteenth century for the Roman rite and that many churches in France, for example, still followed their particular traditions in this matter some hundred years ago. For example, the Curé of Ars purchased a blue vestment for the feasts of the Blessed Virgin; and here and there, an ashen color has been used for Lent, as is done even today in the Ambrosian rite.

Finally, " in particular cases, the matter is to be submitted to the Apostolic See. " The expression, " in particular cases, " should be noted, for it is not only a question of exceptional cases. The poverty of a missionary church or the difficulty which might be encountered in procuring prescribed liturgical vestments can constitute a particular case worthy of the attention of the Apostolic See. Likewise, an exceptional number of priests at the occasion of a Congress would justify a request for dispensing from the chasuble : this dispensation was granted in December, 1964, for the Eucharistic Congress of Bombay. But it is undeniable that, in the present state of things where decisions taken form jurisprudence, competent authority is rather reserved in giving authorizations.

13. The principal celebrant, unless there is some indication to the contrary in the rubrics which follow, accomplishes all the rites and says all the prayers which he himself must accomplish and say ordinarily, according to

the diverse forms of the Mass, when he celebrates alone. Accordingly, he bows, genuflects, kisses the altar, makes the sign of the cross over the oblations and the other gestures in conformity with what is in the rubrics. But he will take care to pronounce the prayers which he must chant or say at the same time as the other concelebrants in a distinct manner and in a voice louder than the other concelebrants, so that all can say each word at the same time with him, especially the words of Consecration, which must be pronounced by all and at the same time, though moral union of the words suffices.

Commentary

The actions and prayers of the concelebrants

The principal celebrant must show in his comportment that it is he who presides over the entire liturgical action. This is why he alone says the presidential prayers, he alone blesses persons and things, he alone carries out most of the ritual gestures.

But the most important element of this article consists in the final words : " the words of Consecration must be pronounced by all at the same time, *though moral union of the words suffices.* " Up to the present, the preoccupation to assure material concommitance of the words of Consecration was for theologians and canonists the essential problem of concelebration : if one of the newly ordained priests should happen to say *Hoc est enim Corpus meum* before the Bishop did so, he would frustrate the latter of his consecration and would become the sole celebrant of the Mass of Ordination ! It was such a fear which made, for example, St. Albert the Great a determined adversary of concelebration. Now, the legislator has given a precision which will liberate fearful consciences; it is inspired from the words of Pius XII on the subject of imposition of hands for the validity of Ordination : " We ordain that, in the bestowing of each Order, the imposition of hands be made in touching physically the head of the ordinand, though *moral contact suffices* for the valid conferral of the Sacrament. " [24]

14. The other concelebrants perform only those gestures and rites expressly assigned to them. They do not extend their hands except when they say aloud either with the principal celebrant or alone those prayers which call for the priest to extend his hands; otherwise, they keep their hands folded. They say aloud only those prayers which they are called upon to say either alone or with the principal celebrant; as far as possible, they should recite them from memory, and should not recite them in a voice so loud that their voice predominates over that of the principal celebrant. As for those prayers whose recitation is not expressly confided to them, they will listen or say them mentally.

Commentary

The rules concerning participation of the other concelebrants in the words and ritual gestures are rather simple : " They perform only those gestures and rites expressly assigned to them, " and " they say aloud only the prayers which they are called upon to say either alone or with the principal celebrant. "

In practice, priests have adopted without difficulty the rule concerning gestures, but a certain number have much trouble conforming to the rule concerning the words : " As for those prayers whose recitation is not expressly confided to them, they will listen, or pray them mentally. " Very often one sees the concelebrants dialoguing the prayers at the foot of the altar, even when the people sing an entrance song; sometimes one sees the lips of the principal celebrant moving while one of the concelebrants reads the *Memento* or the *Communicantes;* the same is true of the other concelebrants during the prayers in preparation

---

[24] Pius XII, apostolic constitution *Sacramentum Ordinis* (November 30, 1947), AAS 40 (1948), p. 7.

for Communion. It is, however, necessary that we come to understand the essentially diversified character of liturgical celebration. It is true that centuries of integral doubling by the celebrant of all the texts read by a minister or sung by the schola have created reflexes which will not be changed in several months. The celebrant had forgotten how to listen, because the rubrics did not leave him a choice. He must learn again to listen : to listen is as sanctifying an action as to speak. It supposes an opening to God who speaks to us with human lips, and an opening to another by whose mouth we pray. To listen demands much interior activity in attention, in faith to the mystery of the Body of Christ in which we are members one of the other. For certain people to listen is an ascesis; for all, this action calls for much charity.

The need of learning to listen for concelebration calls for a word on the ascesis which frequent concelebration demands. Each priest, in offering Mass, adopts a rhythm which is particular to him. Remaining faithful to the smallest details of the *Ritus servandus*, he still marks his celebration with his personality, and no one ought deny him this. However, in concelebration, there is question of a collective rhythm, the blending of one's prayer with that of a confrere who, perhaps, we think, pronounces Latin poorly, who gives a too slow or too rapid cadence for common recitation, who carries out the ritual gestures without grandeur or in a manner a bit theatrical. Even if one had not thought of it at the beginning, it is undeniable that with the demands it makes, concelebration is " formative " and creates unity. While it manifests the unity of the priesthood, it begins by making it a reality in each priestly community which concelebrates.

The last point of the present article should hold our attention : the concelebrants are invited *to recite in as far as possible by memory* the prayers which they are called upon to say alone or with the principal celebrant. On the one hand, indeed, it is not esthetic to place on the altar numerous fascicles of the Canon, in such a way that each concelebrant has one for himself. On the other hand, if the concelebrants not close to the altar hold a book or card in their hands, they cannot recite the Anamnesis with hands extended, as the Ritual prescribes (RC 39 d). In order that the concelebrants can arrive at saying or singing the Canon by heart, it seems necessary that the formula never vary. For this reason it is hoped that, in a later arranging of the rite after the universal experience which is in course now, the *Hanc igitur* will not be recited by all the concelebrants, but only by the principal celebrant.

15. If a priest fills the ministry of a deacon, assistant deacon or subdeacon in a concelebrated Mass, he will abstain from concelebrating at the same Mass.

The deacon, the subdeacon and the assistant deacons may receive Communion under both species; if they are priests, they may receive in this manner even if they have already celebrated Mass or are going to celebrate Mass later.

Commentary

The most perfect form of concelebration at a sung Mass is realized when all the degrees of the hierarchy participate in the course of the liturgy : the Bishop surrounded not only by concelebrating priests, but also with deacons and subdeacons, each exercising the function of his Order, with laymen fulfilling the function of lectors and acolytes when the situation arises.

If it is possible to have a deacon, and not a subdeacon, it is evident that the *missa cum diacono* will be celebrated, and that there will be no idea of having a priest fulfill the function of a deacon while a deacon fulfills that of a subdeacon.

If there is no deacon to participate in the Mass, two solutions present themselves. The first consists in having the ministry of the deacon and subdeacon fulfilled by priests : then these would wear the tunic and dalmatic, but, as the present article recalls, they must clearly abstain from concelebrating at this Mass : they fulfill the purely ministerial functions at the service of the Bishop and the presbyterium.   They can of course receive Communion under both species " even if they have already celebrated Mass or are going to celebrate Mass later, " in order to participate sacramentally at the Sacrifice in which they are ministers; they have presented the gifts at the altar, and those who are fulfilling the deacons' functions will aid in distributing them to the faithful; it is normal that they themselves take part in the table of the Lord.

But such a solution is not the best.   Even though we are accustomed to it in the West, it is not normal that a priest wear the insignia of a deacon : he could be leading the people into error regarding his person.   Furthermore, the priests designated to fulfill these ministerial functions are in appearance excluded from the unity of the presbyterium, of which concelebration is the sign.   Since " it is permitted to Bishops, according to need, to celebrate sung Mass in the manner of priests " (I 48), it is better to invite all the priests to concelebrate around the Bishop according to the rite of a sung Mass, where the Epistle will be proclaimed by a lector (RC 85) and the Gospel by one of the concelebrants (RC 86).   The diversity of functions is not incompatible with the respect of the truth of the hierarchical order in which each individual finds himself.

16. The deacon, subdeacon and other ministers and servants will take care not to stand among the concelebrants, except when their service is called for according to the rubrics; when their services have been accomplished, they will return to their places as soon as possible.

Commentary

This prescription was already formulated for the deacon and the subdeacon in the *Ritus servandus in celebratione*

Missae (RS 69), but it should constitute the golden rule of masters of ceremonies and take the first place in their customs. It descends in a straight line from the Roman ceremonial of 1516, according to which the master of ceremonies *ad Summum Pontificem non accedat sine urgenti causa, vel nisi vocatus*. [25] No one is unaware of how much the situation has deteriorated in this domain since the sixteenth century, the masters of ceremonies having become omnipresent personages. The putting into practice of the Ordo of concelebration should lead them to reflect on their functions and the manner of carrying them out. The best are those who know how to prepare with utmost care the rites before their execution, leaving nothing to improvisation, and who know best how to make themselves forgotten during the celebration.

What Must be Prepared

17. Besides what is required for any Mass, the following will be prepared :

a) all the liturgical vestments which the principal celebrant must wear, according to the different forms of Mass;

b) amice, alb, cincture, maniple, stole and chasuble for each of the concelebrants;

c) one host sufficiently large, or several according to the number of concelebrants, which will later be broken into particles, and hosts for the Communion of the faithful. If the Communion of the concelebrants is to be given by intinction, care is to be taken that the hosts are not too small or too thin, but somewhat thicker than usual so that, after having been partially dipped in the Precious Blood, they can be distributed conveniently;

d) one chalice sufficiently large; or, if it is not possible to have such a one, a second so that it can suffice for the Communion of all the concelebrants;

---

[25] *Sacrarum caeremoniarum* S. R. E., liber 3, cap. 4.

e) a burse with corporal, or, if necessary, several corporals, a pall and purificator for the chalice, as well as other purificators for the concelebrants;

f) patens for the Communion of the concelebrants;

g) silver straws or silver spoons for each of the concelebrants, and a vessel with water to purify them, if the Precious Blood is to be taken with straw or spoon;

h) booklets with the Ordinary of the Mass, if necessary, for the concelebrants;

i) one or several vessels with water for purifying the fingers;

j) chairs or benches for the concelebrants, close to the chair of the principal celebrant, or in some other suitable place in the sanctuary.

Commentary

Not all of the ten paragraphs in this article call for a special commentary; a few call for an explanation.

a) In speaking of the liturgical vestments which the principal celebrant must wear *according to the different forms of the Mass*, the reference is to Masses celebrated by a Bishop. While a priest always wears the same vestments for Mass, whether it be read or sung, the Bishop normally wears the *pontificalia* when he celebrates according to the solemn form.

b) There is no doubt that having one bread is an intimate part of the Eucharistic symbolism: *there is one sole bread; and therefore, though numerous, we are one body, all of us who have part in the one bread and the one chalice* (I Cor. 10 : 17). The breaking of the bread receives its significance when one bread is broken and shared. While the number of communicants does not usually allow for one bread which the priest and faithful share, concelebration allows the manifestation of this sign in the Communion of the priests.

Clearly, a Eucharistic bread sufficiently large ought to be thicker than the usual hosts. Also, there must be thicker breads than usual when Communion is given by intinction, for the bread must conserve its consistency when it is dipped in the consecrated Wine. In fact, the needs of concelebration and Communion under both species have led some religious communities which make altarbreads to reconsider their techniques of fabrication. For a long time, it has been remarked that the thin hosts, white and little, do not leave even a chance to feel the taste of bread when they are consumed. The sign of bread was thus reduced to its simplest expression and obviously created difficulty in the instruction of children. Now, when Canon Law (CIC 816) and the Roman missal [26] imposed the use of unleavened bread in the celebration of the Eucharist in the Latin rite, they did not intend to impose the eating of bread without taste and of a whiteness of a sheet of paper. Thus each day grows the number of churches which use a larger and thicker bread which the present article recommends for concelebration.

Sometimes, objections arise concerning unleavened bread in the new form : some feel that it leaves too many crumbs and they wonder if it conserves as well as the other. To the first objection it can be answered that the bread which the Lord used, when He instituted the Eucharist, must surely have left crumbs, but also that we must look for a new form of paten; we have need of patens which are larger and deeper, similar to those left us by the Middle Ages that today we admire in museums. In these larger and rather deep patens it would be easy to carry out the breaking of the bread and to gather the crumbs, which flat patens do not retain. As for the second objection, it is not borne out by experience : the thicker hosts, fabricated according to a process of appropriate cooking, do not corrupt more quickly than the others; they can be conserved for at least two months. Furthermore, it should be recalled that the Eucharistic

---

[26] Roman Missal, on errors in the celebration, 5.

Reserve need not be abundant, for the priest will normally consecrate at each Mass the particles which will be distributed to the faithful at the time of Communion.

c) One chalice is called for by the same reasoning as that of the one bread, and it corresponds to Roman tradition, as we have seen above (p. 41). Therefore, care should be taken that this be respected each time it is possible to do so. Here again, it is to be hoped that chalicemakers will reflect on the new forms which concelebration calls for. The chalices with handles of ancient times can perhaps suggest the chalices of tomorrow : in the Mass celebrated facing the people, such chalices would give much nobility to the rite of the Elevation. The form of ciboria will without doubt also evolve. Ciboria have taken on the form of a chalice with a cover, but this is not really normal : one does not put bread in a table glass. It would be more fitting to have the ciborium like a deep platter or a large cup without stand.

d) It is not so necessary to have as many purificators as concelebrants; the dignity of the rite calls for a limitation of impedimenta.

e) Several patens will be necessary for the breaking of the bread and for Communion if this is done by intinction. When Communion is given under both species separately, the use of the individual paten is facultative : when the concelebrants have received the Body of Christ from the hands of the Bishop, or have taken it themselves from the altar, they hold it with the right hand " over a paten *or over the left hand* " (RC 47). The practice of holding the consecrated bread with the right hand and of making a " throne " with the left hand was already tradition in Jerusalem in the middle of the fourth century (above, p. 47). Many prefer to be inspired by this rather than use the paten.

f) The placing of the chairs of the concelebrants clearly depends on the place. While ancient Roman basilicas offer an ideal disposition with the cathedra of the Bishop arranged in an apse without depth, with on either side in a semi-circle the benches of the concelebrating priests, it is not necessary to have the same arrangement everywhere. When the principal celebrant is a priest and not a Bishop, it is not fitting that he occupy a place too elevated in relation to those of his colleagues. Likewise, in monastic or religious choirs, it may often be necessary for the concelebrants to take their place as usual in the choir stalls for the Liturgy of the Word, in order to sing the Proper.

When possible, care should be taken that the principal celebrant appear at one and the same time the president of the assembly and the first member of the presbyterium. His seat should not therefore be placed too far from the other concelebrants. It is not indispensible that each of these have an individual seat. At the papal chapel, the Cardinals in cappa, chasuble or dalmatic, occupy simple stools. One might find example in this placement for concelebration.

Rite for the Pontifical Mass

1. PREPARATION

18. The Bishop who is principal celebrant puts on in the sacristy the liturgical vestments which he habitually wears when he celebrates a pontifical Mass. The other concelebrants wear the liturgical vestments which are proper to them.

It is also in the sacristy that the deacon, subdeacon and the other ministers vest as usual; so also the assistant deacons, though at a concelebrated Mass two of the concelebrants may fulfil their functions.

Commentary

First to be noted is that the vesting of the Bishop and the concelebrants is to take place in the sacristy and not in the sanctuary. Note also that there is question here neither of the singing of Terce or another Hour of the Office, nor of the recitation of the prayers for the preparation of Mass. Regarding these two points, the rite of concelebration does no more than conform itself to the regulation established by the Ordo of Holy Week (1955).

If several deacons participate at the concelebration, it is normal that three of them assist the Bishop : two at the throne, the other at the altar. But it is not fitting that dignitaries put on dalmatics to fulfil the function of assisting deacons; it is better for two concelebrating priests to assist the Bishop at the throne.

19. The office of assistant-priest is filled by one of the concelebrating priests who, however, does not wear a cope, but the chasuble and all the other priestly vestments.

Commentary

From the point of view of dignity, the assistant-priest is the first of the concelebrating priests. But his role at the altar being to assist the Bishop in the service of the book, he normally will take his place at the left of the Bishop.

By way of the practice of concelebration, Roman tradition is restored in that which concerns the vesting of the assistant-priest : he has returned to the chasuble in conformity with the ancient *Ordines*. The custom of having him wear a cope was of Germanic origin. [27]

2. THE LITURGY OF THE WORD

The Beginning of the Mass

20. When all has been prepared, the Bishop who is principal celebrant places and blesses the incense, and the procession which goes through the church to the altar is arranged in the following way : the thurifer with the censer smoking; a subdeacon with the processional cross between acolytes carrying lighted candles; the clergy, if present; then, the subdeacon carrying the Book of the Gospels; the concelebrating priests and concelebrating Bishops; the assistant-priest with the deacon at his left; and finally, the Bishop principal celebrant, with two assistant deacons or two concelebrants at his side.

While the procession goes through the church, the entrance antiphon with its psalm is sung.

21. When they have arrived at the altar, the concelebrants, having made the required reverence, ascend the altar two by two and kiss it; then they take the places assigned to them.

Commentary

It might be better that the kissing of the altar by the concelebrants not be obligatory in all circumstances.

---

[27] Ordo Romanus X, 3 (*Ordo Missae* of the Romano-Germanic Pontifical of the middle of the 10th century), M. Andrieu, *op. cit.*, II, p. 351.

When, in a monastic church, the concelebrants must sing the Introit in the entrance procession, it would be better that they gain their places directly in entering the choir, as is their custom each time they take part in a procession.

22. **The Bishop principal celebrant, having made his reverence to the altar, says in a subdued voice together with his ministers the prayers at the foot of the altar; then the Mass continues as usual, observing however all that follows.**

Commentary

The Bishops' Ceremonial wishes that, for the prayers at the foot of the altar, the subdeacon confide the Book of the Gospels to the master of ceremonies (CE lib. 2, cap. 8, 30). Would it not be better that he go up and place it on the altar when he arrives? In any case, when the Bishop has kissed the book after having venerated the altar, the Gospel Book must remain at the center of the altar, until the deacon goes to take it for the proclamation of the Gospel.

23. **The Book of the Gospels is left on the altar, at the center, after the Bishop principal celebrant has kissed the altar and the Gospel Book.**

The Readings

24. **If there are other readings before the Epistle, the lector once the oration is finished, having made, when required, the proper reverences to the altar and to the Bishop, goes to the ambo or to another suitable place, and there, facing the people, he sings or recites the reading.**

25. **For reading the Epistle, the subdeacon, once the oration is finished, takes the book, and after having made, if need be, the required reverences to the altar and to the Bishop, he goes to the ambo or another suitable place and there, facing the people, he sings or reads the Epistle. Afterwards, he goes before the Bishop and, bowing, receives from him his blessing.**

26. At the proper time, the deacon, having made the required reverences, goes to the altar, and kneeling on the bottom step, says in a low voice the Munda cor meum; then he takes the Book of the Gospels from the altar. During this time, the Bishop places and blesses the incense; this done, the thurifer, acolytes and subdeacon, in the usual way, escort the deacon carrying the Book in such as way as to honor it. The deacon comes before the Bishop and, bowing, asks his blessing; then he goes to the ambo or other suitable place and there, facing the people, he sings or reads the Gospel.

27. After the homily, the absolution is not given.

Commentary

This article may seem enigmatic to more than one reader. In fact, in France, for example, no church seems to have kept the custom of an absolution after the homily. According to the Ceremonial, the deacon, at the end of the sermon, recites the *Confiteor*, then the assistant-priest proclaims the indulgences after which the Bishop gives the absolution (CE lib. 3, cap. 8, 50). This rite, of German origin, was already in use at Rome in the middle of the twelfth century [28] and Durand of Mende speaks of it in his Pontifical. [29] In the sixteenth century, it was not reserved to the Bishop's Mass; certain editions of the *Ritus servandus* of the missal of St. Pius V give the formulary for a Mass sung by a priest. [30]

Some have tried to see in this practice a penitential rite preparing for the Eucharistic Liturgy. It seems, however, that it is to be attached to the preaching. In fact, it always

---

[28] *Ordo officiorum ecclesiae lateranensis* of Canon Bernhard, 176; ed. L. Fischer (Munich 1916), p. 82. *Liber politicus* of Canon Bento, 20, ed. Mabillon (Ordo 11), PL 78, col. 1033.

[29] M. Andrieu, *op. cit.*, III : " Le Pontifical de Guillaume Durand, " p. 639.

[30] Castellani, *Sacerdotale*, ed. 1579, p. 80.

followed immediately, whether this was done before the singing of the *Credo* or after the presentation of the gifts

28. After the Creed, the Bishop principal celebrant says Dominus vobiscum and Oremus, and the Prayer of the Faithful takes place, according to the custom of the place

3. THE EUCHARISTIC LITURGY

The Offertory

29. When the Offertory antiphon is begun, the offerings are carried to the altar by the ministers and all is carried out as usual for the Offertory. If the faithful offer gifts, the Bishop principal celebrant receives them at the sanctuary gates, assisted, if there is need, by some of the concelebrants. After this, he washes his hands.

Then the Bishop principal celebrant, together with the other concelebrants, goes to the altar, makes the required reverences and with the assistant-priest ascends the altar which he kisses. The other concelebrants, after having made the required reverence, stand on the floor around the altar, but in such a way as not to interfere with the Offertory rite. If it seems fitting, the concelebrants may come to the altar before the principal celebrant sings the Prayer over the Gifts.

Commentary

The Ritual foresees three possible places for the concelebrants during the Mass : first, during the Liturgy of the Word, and then after having received Communion, they remain at their places, sitting or standing; second, during the beginning of the Offertory, they take their places in the sanctuary *in plano* at the foot of the altar; finally, before the Prayer over the Gifts, they approach the altar.

For the second part, which is described here, it is evident that consideration must be taken of the disposition of the place and of ceremonial needs. Thus, for example the direct approaches to the altar must, in any hypothesis be free to permit the circular incensing of the altar.   So also, the ministers of the Bishop, the deacon and subdeacon, the thurifer, the acolytes presenting the water and hand towel at the *Lavabo*, the cleric charged with the miter, as well as the master of ceremonies must be able to fulfill easily their functions in relation to the Bishop.

The Ritual allows, however, " if it seems suitable, " that this intermediate part be omitted and all the concelebrants approach the altar at the beginning of the Offertory. Its intention is to offer great freedom to permit the adaptation of the rites to local conditions, but it would not often be suitable to make use of this possibility because of the incensing which would lack dignity if the steps of the altar were already occupied on three sides.

30.   All the prayers of the Offertory are said silently by the Bishop principal celebrant alone.

Commentary

The prayers of the Offertory which precede the Prayer over the Gifts are private prayers of the celebrant.   He must not therefore give them a community importance by raising his voice at all.   If one or the other concelebrant wishes to say them personally, he is to do so mentally (RC 14).

The *Orate Fratres* and the *Suscipiat* are part of the private prayers of the Offertory.   This is the reason why the French Bishops did not wish to have them said in the vernacular. The *Ordo Missae* declares that they are to be said in a voice (tone) that is fitting, *congrua voce* (OM 29).   At the solemn Mass, it is in a low voice that the celebrant will say them and the ministers will respond in a similar way.   In any case, it is not fitting that the concelebrants recite the *Suscipiat*.

31.   The concelebrants are incensed once as a group, immediately after the Bishop principal celebrant.

Commentary

All the concelebrants are incensed together *per modum unius*, and this includes the assistant-priest.

32.   Before the Bishop principal celebrant sings the Prayer over the Gifts, the concelebrants, if they are not too numerous and if the size of the altar permits it, take place around the table of the altar; otherwise, they take their places in the most convenient place around the altar, but in such a way that the rite can easily be seen by the faithful and that the deacon can approach the altar and the Bishop when this is necessary.

Commentary

In placing the concelebrants around the altar, care must be taken above all that " the rite be seen easily by the faithful. " The Ritual has already indicated one of the conditions for visibility of the rite : " the concelebrants should not stand at the side of the altar which faces the people " (RC 4) and we have underlined the pastoral importance of respecting this regulation (above, p. 42).

33.   The assisting deacons and the subdeacon stand on the floor; the deacon remains behind the Bishop principal celebrant, and he ascends to the altar when he must accomplish his service in regard to the chalice.

Commentary

The rule given here does not introduce an innovation in relation to the Ritual of concelebration of the Mass, which calls for the deacon to stand behind the celebrant, approach the altar to carry out his ministry, and immediately return to his place (RS 69). As for the assisting deacons and the subdeacon, it was always a rule that they remain *in plano* during the Canon. They come to the altar only to receive Communion.

34.   The Prayer over the Gifts is sung by the Bishop principal celebrant alone, in the oration tone, up to and including the words Per omnia saecula saeculorum.

Commentary

The Bishop should wait for all the concelebrants to arrive at their places around the altar before beginning the singing of the Prayer over the Gifts.

The Canon

35. The Bishop principal celebrant alone sings the dialogue before the Preface, to which all respond, and the Preface itself; the Sanctus is sung by all the concelebrants together with the people and the schola.

Commentary

The singing of the *Sanctus* by all the concelebrants, the clergy and the people imposes the choice of a simple melody well-known. With the Gregorian melodies XIII and especially XVIII of the Roman Kyriale, it is easy to find a united and triumphal chant for the assembly in Latin. For the singing in the vernacular, it is to be hoped that agreement will soon be reached for one or two melodies, so that these can be learned in all parishes and that everywhere the assembly can continue to sing the *Sanctus*. It would be contrary to the spirit of the conciliar reform that the use of the language of the land have as a result the reducing of a part of the people to silence. While it is allowed that research continue regarding the other chants of the Ordinary, the *Sanctus* should never be the subject of any yielding in the principle of communal singing.

36. After the singing of the Sanctus has been completed, the concelebrants will continue the Canon in the manner indicated below. However, only the Bishop principal celebrant makes the gestures, unless there is a contrary indication.

37. The Te igitur is said aloud by the Bishop principal celebrant alone.

38. The Memento of the living and the Communicantes may be given by the Bishop principal celebrant to one or two of the concelebrants, who alone will say these prayers with hands extended.

Commentary

If the *Memento* of the living and the *Communicantes* are to be given to one or the other of the concelebrants, it is evident that the division should be made before the beginning of the Mass and not at the moment of the reading of the diptychs (above, pp. 90-91).

It does not seem desirable that the *Memento* and the *Communicantes* be said by only one of the concelebrants because, in the eyes of the faithful, this one would assume a place more important than that of the principal celebrant in the recitation of the Canon.

39. From the Hanc igitur to the Supplices inclusive, all the concelebrants together sing the prayers or recite them aloud, in the following manner :

a) Hanc igitur with hands extended toward the offerings, and folded at the words Per Christum Dominum nostrum;

b) Quam oblationem, Qui pridie, Simili modo, hands folded, and bowing the head at the words gratias agens;

c) the words of Consecration, the right hand extended toward the bread and the chalice, if this seems suitable; at the elevation, looking at the host and the chalice, and afterwards bowing profoundly;

d) Unde et memores and Supra quae with hands extended;

e) Supplices, bowed profoundly and hands folded just up to the words ex hac altaris participatione and then standing straight and signing themselves at the words omni benedictione caelesti et gratia repleamur.

Commentary

" From the *Hanc igitur* to the *Supplices te rogamus* inclusive, all the concelebrants sing or recite aloud these prayers. "

The rubric which precedes the two melodies of the Canon allows great liberty in the determining of the extent of the singing : one can sing the entire formulary or only the recital of the Institution of the Eucharist *(Qui pridie, Simili modo,* and *Haec quotiescumque feceritis); one can even limit the singing to the words of Consecration. Experience has shown that the singing of the ensemble of the formulary can be tiring. In a certain number of communities, the concelebrants sing only the recital of the Institution and the Anamnesis *(Unde et memores),* which is thus given importance. Whatever be the extent of the part of the Canon sung, we cannot insist too much on its pastoral value (above, p. 43).

The gestures of the concelebrants during the Canon are described with clarity. However, the Ritual omits to say that, in the prayer *Supplices te rogamus,* the concelebrants who are standing around the table of the altar kiss it at the same time as does the principal celebrant, after having said the words *ut quotquot* according to the rubric of the Canon of the Mass which follows the Ritual of concelebration (p. 195).

The paragraph concerning the Consecration calls for some explanations. We read there that, during the words of Consecration, the concelebrants may hold " the right hand extended toward the bread and the chalice, if this seems suitable. " What is the significance of this gesture? Is it a demonstrative gesture or rather a gesture restored in reference to the *Apostolic Tradition* of Hippolytus? He prescribes : " Let the Bishop, in imposing hands (over the oblation) *with all the presbyterium,* say in giving thanks : The Lord be with you. " [31] In the explanation

---

[31] *La Tradition apostolique de saint Hippolyte,* 4; ed. B. Botte (Münster 1963), p. 11. The documents which depend on the Apostolic Tradition hand on the same description : The *Testament of the Lord,* lib. 1, 25, ed. I. E. Rahmani, *Testamentum DNIC* (Mainz 1899), p. 37; the *Canons of Hippolytus,* 3 (" he who has become bishop imposes *his*

of the documents which they propose unofficially the *Notitiae* of the Liturgical Commission think that here we have a demonstrative gesture and that the palm of the hand should not be turned toward the ground, but to the side. [32]   To this interpretation we can object that this demonstrative gesture would constitute a unique instance in the Roman Liturgy and especially that, in the thinking of the promoters of this rite, it concerns a *signum significationis et consecrationis per operationem Spiritus Sancti.* From this, evidently, it would be necessary for the hand to be turned not to the side but downward. Since it concerns an important gesture, though facultative, it is indispensable that competent authority give an official interpretation.

For the double Elevation, the concelebrants should take care that all bow and rise together. To arrive at this the best would be to conform to the following rule, which is inspired from the rubric for the Canon of concelebration (p. 193) : all look at the host at the moment when the principal celebrant shows it to the people; when the priest begins to lower his arms to place the Host down on the altar, each of the concelebrants bows profoundly up to the moment when the celebrant makes his genuflection; all straighten up at the same time as he. The same is to be done for the chalice.

40. The Memento **of the dead and the** Nobis quoque peccatoribus **can be given by the Bishop principal celebrant to one or the other of the concelebrants, who alone says these prayers aloud and with hands extended.**

At the words Nobis quoque peccatoribus, **each concelebrant strikes his breast.**

---

hand on the offerings with the priests "), ed. R. Coquin, mimeographed thesis (Paris 1962), p. 9. See also the painting coming from the cemetery of Callixtus reproduced in G. Wilpert, *Le Pitture delle Catacombe romane* (Rome 1903), volume of illustrations, p. 41, reproduction 1.

[32] *Notitiae, Commentarii ad nuntia de re liturgica edenda cura Consilii ad exsequendam Constitutionem de sacra Liturgia,* 1 (1965), p. 143.

Commentary

One can but repeat here what has been said in the commentary on article 38.

41. The Per quem haec omnia is said by the Bishop principal celebrant alone, while the others stand with their hands folded.

42. The final Doxology of the Canon, from the words Per ipsum to Per omnia saecula saeculorum inclusive, is sung or said by all the concelebrants together with the Bishop principal celebrant.

Commentary

It is curious that the Ritual of concelebration leaves a choice between the singing and the recitation of the final Doxology of the Canon at solemn Mass, while the singing of the Embolism of the Lord's Prayer is obligatory (RC 44). It is surely fitting that the *Per ipsum* be offered in the same fashion as the Preface and hence that it be sung by all the concelebrants at a sung Mass, even if the central part of the Canon was only recited. The singing of the *Per ipsum* is not a particularity of concelebration, but was instituted by the Instruction *Inter Oecumenici* (I 48 f) and has found place in the *Ordo Missae*.

Preparation for Communion

43. The Bishop principal celebrant sings the admonition before the Lord's Prayer, and then, with the other concelebrants, the Lord's Prayer itself.

Commentary

The Ritual makes no allusion to the gestures of the Bishop and the other concelebrants during the singing of the Lord's Prayer. These ought then to conform to general norms : the Bishop extending his hands, as at Mass when he celebrates alone (RC 13), while the other concelebrants keep their hands folded (RC 14).

44.   The Libera nos is sung by the Bishop principal celebrant alone who, at the conclusion of the prayer, breaks the host and drops a particle into the chalice, as usual.

45.   During the singing of the Agnus Dei, if several hosts must be broken for the Communion of the concelebrants, the Bishop principal celebrant breaks the hosts with the aid of one another of the concelebrants closest to him.

Commentary

In order that the concelebrants closest to the Bishop can aid him in the breaking of the bread, it is indispensable that this rite be carried out not over the chalice but over one or several of the patens.   In the seventh century, at Rome, the breaking of the bread was a rite in which the entire presbyterium participated : while the Pope broke the bread over a paten, the priests broke it in sacks which the acolytes presented to them. [33]   The breaking of the bread lost much of its importance with the increasing rarity of Communion of the faithful and the spreading of the custom of particles cut in advance.   But in the thirteenth century, according to the Ordo of the Roman Curia, the celebrant always continued to break the bread over the paten. [34]   This is a natural gesture : at table one breaks bread over a plate and not over one's glass.

46.   After the breaking of the hosts, the Bishop principal celebrant alone says silently the prayer Domine Jesu Christe, qui dixisti; then he kisses the altar and gives the kiss of peace to the concelebrants and after them to the assisting deacons unless they are to receive Communion.

---

[33] Ordo Romanus I, 101-104 in M. Andrieu, *op. cit.*, II, p. 100.

[34] Cod. Vat. Ottobon. lat. 356, ed. J. Brinktrine, *Ephemerides Liturgicae* 51 (1937), p. 206.

If the concelebrants are not too numerous, each of them
may come to the Bishop principal celebrant and receive
from him the kiss of peace, omitting, however, the genuflection and the kissing of the altar. But, if the number of
concelebrants is great, the Bishop principal celebrant
gives the kiss of peace only to the two concelebrants at his
right and left; these, in turn, give the kiss of peace to the
concelebrants nearest them and so on in order. Then
the Bishop principal celebrant alone says silently the
prayers Domine Jesu Christe Fili Dei vivi and Perceptio.
The kiss of peace is given to those in the choir by the
assistant priest in the usual manner.

Commentary

As the *Ordo Missae* prescribes, the Bishop says the prayer
for peace immediately after the breaking of the bread,
without reciting the *Agnus Dei*, which is sung by the
people (OM 49). The kiss of peace should not take too
long a time. Thus, the second solution proposed by the
Ritual will often be adopted, even if the number of
concelebrants is not considerable. The assisting deacons,
the deacon of the altar and the subdeacon do not receive
the kiss of peace if they are going to receive Communion;
it is after having presented to each of these the Body
of Christ that the Bishop will give them the kiss of peace,
in agreement with the Ceremonial (CE lib. 2, cap. 29, 3).
Let us recall, finally, that the principal celebrant alone
recites silently the two prayers of preparation, as well
as the *Panem caelestem, Domine non sum dignus* and *Corpus
Domini nostri* (RC 47). If the other concelebrants wish
to say them for themselves, they may do so mentally
(RC 14).

Communion of the Lord's Body

47. When the prayers before Communion have been said,
the Bishop principal celebrant genuflects, says silently
the Panem caelestem accipiam and retires a bit, to the
left side.

The other concelebrants come one by one to the center of the altar, genuflect, and, if they are Bishops, themselves take the Lord's Body from the altar; if they are priests, they receive it from the Bishop principal celebrant; and holding the host in the right hand over a paten or over their left hand, they return to their places around the altar. However, if it seems more suitable, even the concelebrants who are not Bishops may take directly from the altar the Lord's Body. When all have the Lord's Body, the Bishop principal celebrant takes his particle at his turn, and, bowed, he says as usual three times the Domine non sum dignus and Corpus Domini nostri and all, bowed, reverently receive the Body of the Lord.

48. If the principal celebrant is a prelate without the episcopal character, the concelebrating priests take the Body of the Lord directly from the altar.

49. If the number of concelebrants is great, the Bishop principal celebrant may be aided by one or another of the concelebrants, if necessary, to carry to each of the concelebrants who remain at their place the Body of the Lord; these, standing, receive it in their right hand over a paten or over the left hand. All else is done as described above. Nothing prevents the Bishop principal celebrant from giving the particles placed on a paten to the first concelebrant, or again to each of those who are next to him; this one takes his particle and then gives the paten to the next one and so on until the last. When all have taken in their hand the Body of the Lord, all is done as has been described above.

50. When the concelebrants have received the Communion of the Body of the Lord, the assisting deacons, and after them, the deacon and subdeacon come forward and receive Communion from the Bishop principal celebrant in the usual manner, and, then, the kiss of peace.

Commentary

The Ritual of concelebration offers very fluid rules, because of the diversity of situations created by the number of concelebrants and the importance of the assembly who will receive Communion. We would like to clarify these regulations by relating them to some general principles.

1. *The Moment of the Communion of the Concelebrants*

We must distinguish between the moment when each concelebrant receives the Body of Christ and the moment when all together communicate.

The receiving of the Body of Christ takes place after the Bishop has said silently the *Panem caelestem accipiam* and before he says the *Domine non sum dignus*. However, if the principal celebrant is going to distribute Communion to the faithful after he has received from the chalice, he takes a particle *before the concelebrants receive the Body of Christ*, " showing it to the faithful, saying : *Ecce Agnus Dei*, and, then, with the concelebrants and the faithful, says three times : *Domine non sum dignus* aloud " (RC 58).

The consuming of the Body of Christ is done together : " When all have the Body of Christ in their hands, the Bishop principal celebrant takes his particle in his turn, and then, bowed, he says as usual three times : *Domine non sum dignus (unless he has already said it with the people in the case foreseen above)* and *Corpus Domini nostri*, and all, bowed, consume reverently the Body of the Lord " (RC 47). However, " one can also arrange the Communion of the concelebrants in such a way that each of them receives the Body of the Lord over the altar and immediately after receives the Blood of the Lord " (RC 56).

2. *The Minister of the Body of the Lord*

The distribution of the Body of Christ is a service in which is affirmed once more the hierarchical character of the Church. When concelebration is presided over by a Bishop, it is he who gives the consecrated Bread to the concelebrating priests.

Tradition is unanimous in affirming that the Bishop is, in relation to priests, the minister of the Body of Christ. In the most ancient texts, we see the Bishop distributing the Eucharist to the entire assembly : " When he has broken the bread, in presenting each piece he will say : ' The bread of heaven in Christ Jesus. ' And he who receives answers : ' Amen. ' " [35] One can also refer to the witness of the Oriental Syrian Liturgy and to that of the *Liber Pontificalis* cited above (p. 16 and 21). Here, in the concelebration of the Syrian type, the Bishop has a priest say the consecratory Anaphora, but he gives himself Communion and then distributes the consecrated bread to the other concelebrants.

But while the Bishop is the minister of the Body of Christ in regard to priests, he is not so in relation to the other concelebrating Bishops : these " take directly the Body of the Lord from the altar " (RC 47). However, at Rome, in the seventh century, the Pope himself gave the bread to the Bishops who concelebrated with him : *accedunt primum episcopi ad sedem, ut communicent de manu pontificis secundum ordinem.* [36]

Only the Bishop is minister of the Body of Christ in relation to priests; the priest celebrant is not so in relation to his colleagues, even if he has some special dignity (RC 48).

3.   *Manner of Distributing the Body of the Lord*

In discussing the distribution of the Body of Christ one must distinguish two cases, according as the principal celebrant is a Bishop or a priest.

When the principal celebrant is a Bishop, four ways of distributing the Body of Christ are possible.

---

[35] *La Tradition apostolique,* 21, ed. B. Botte, *op. cit.,* p. 57.

[36] Ordo Romanus I, 108 in M. Andrieu, *op. cit.,* II, p. 102.

The Bishop himself may give the consecrated bread to each of the priest concelebrants : the priest concelebrants " come one by one to the center of the altar, genuflect, and receive the Body of the Lord from the Bishop principal celebrant; holding it in the right hand over a paten or over the left hand, they return to their places around the altar " (RC 47). This is clearly the manner of Communion most conforming to tradition and that which best shows the Bishop as the president of the Eucharistic table, " the faithful and prudent steward whom the master has placed at the head of his household to give to each his ration of grain in due time, " as we read in the Communion antiphon at the Mass of holy Bishops (from Lk. 12 : 42).

The Bishop may be aided in the distribution of the consecrated bread : " if the number of concelebrants is great, the Bishop principal celebrant may be aided by one or another of the concelebrants, if necessary, to carry the Body of the Lord to each of the concelebrants who remain at their places " (RC 49).   In this case, the Bishop takes a paten and he himself goes to give the consecrated bread to each of the concelebrants or only to some of them, the others being served by one or other priest, who will have received from the hand of the Bishop the paten filled with particles.

The Bishop may give a paten filled with particles to a concelebrating priest close to him or to two priests who are near him in an immediate manner : " This one takes his particle and then gives the paten to the next one and so on until the last " (RC 49).

The fourth manner of distributing the Body of Christ does not put in relief the specific ministry of the Bishop : " if it seems more suitable, " the concelebrating priests may " take directly from the altar the Body of the Lord, " as they do when the principal celebrant is not a Bishop (RC 47). Such a solution should not be adopted unless it really seems suitable.   Usually, one of the three other possibilities would be chosen.

4.   *Communion of Concelebrants in the Absence of a Bishop*

If we were to hold to the letter of the Ritual, only a concelebration presided over by a Bishop would offer to the concelebrants the choice of different manners of receiving Communion of the Body of Christ which we have described.   In fact, article 48 declares : " If the principal celebrant is a prelate without the episcopal character, the concelebrating priests take the Body of the Lord directly from the altar; " and in the explanation of the rites of solemn Mass, sung Mass and recited Mass we find repeated : " For the preparation of Communion as well as for the ceremonial to be observed at this time where it deals with the Communion of concelebrants and ministers or the faithful, all is to be observed which is found in numbers 43-58, *with the exclusion of rites proper to the pontifical Mass* " (RC 75, 92, 107).

It does not seem, however, to have been the will of the legislator to impose a frame too rigid for concelebration by priests.   The different ways of Communion which are set forth in the description of the pontifical Mass can certainly be used in the absence of a Bishop, with the exception of the first : the concelebrating priests will not come one by one to receive the consecrated bread from the hand of the principal celebrant who is not a Bishop, since this manner is proper to a Mass presided over by a Bishop.

5.   *The Communion of the Sacred Ministers*

The two assisting deacons, the deacon and the subdeacon receive the Body of Christ from the hand of the Bishop before he receives Communion from the chalice.   This is an innovation in relation to the rites of celebration of Mass (RS 83).   It is justified by the fact that the ministers must normally receive Communion in the Blood of the Lord immediately afterwards.

The regulation of the Ceremonial according to which the Bishop gives the kiss of peace to each of the four ministers after having given them the Eucharist has been kept. This practice was unknown to ancient Roman tradition. Its oldest witness seems to be furnished by the Germanic ordinals of the end of the ninth and the beginning of the tenth century. In this epoch, the Bishop gave this kiss of communion to priests and deacons and the kiss immediately preceded Communion. [37] In the twelfth century, the practice was received at Rome. [38] In his tract on the mystery of the altar (around 1198), Pope Innocent III explains why the priests and deacons receive the kiss from the Pontiff at Communion, while the subdeacon does not receive it. [39] The present practice was certainly not codified before the papal Ceremonial of 1485. One could therefore abandon it without renouncing a tradition characteristic of the Roman rite.

Communion with the Chalice

51. Communion from the chalice may be received by drinking directly from one and the same chalice, or with a straw, or with a spoon, or even by dipping the host in the Precious Blood.

Commentary

The Ritual distinguishes four types of Communion with the chalice. It would be more exact to speak of Communion of the Blood of Christ, for Communion by intinction is not a Communion from the chalice, because the celebrant only dips the consecrated bread in the wine before placing it in the mouth of the communicant.

---

[37] Ordo Romanus IX, 42 and Ordo Romanus X, 59 in M. Andrieu, *op. cit.*, II, p. 335 and 361.

[38] *Ordo officiorum ecclesiae lateranensis*, 178, *op. cit.*, p. 85.

[39] Innocent III, *De sacro altaris mysterio*, lib. 6, cap. 9.

1.   *Communion directly from the chalice*

52. If Communion is received directly from the chalice, the procedure is as follows : the Bishop principal celebrant says silently the Quid retribuam... and then takes the chalice and, without making the sign of the cross, says silently the Sanguis Domini nostri, drinks a little of the consecrated wine and gives the chalice to the deacon.

The deacon wipes the exterior of the chalice with a purificator; then he places himself at the center or at the right of the altar, i.e., there where he can most conveniently present the chalice to the other concelebrants. If the deacon stands at the right side, a second corporal should be placed on the altar there.

The concelebrants approach one by one and, without genuflecting, each receives the chalice from the deacon, and holding it together with the deacon, if this can be done conveniently, and placing the purificator under his mouth, he drinks a little of the consecrated wine; afterwards, he washes his hands at the credence table and returns to his place as at the beginning of the Mass. After the Communion of each of the concelebrants the deacon wipes the exterior of the chalice.

The assisting deacons and the subdeacon come last to receive the consecrated wine; and when the deacon says to them, Sanguis Christi, they respond Amen. Then the deacon himself receives Communion and consumes all the consecrated wine that remains. He carries the chalice to a table near the altar and there he purifies it; the subdeacon wipes and arranges the chalice as usual.

Commentary

The most traditional way of receiving Communion of the Blood of Christ is that which consists in drinking the consecrated wine by bringing to the lips the chalice which the deacon presents (above, p. 48). It is one of the values of the Ritual of concelebration and that of Communion under both species to have restored the ministerial function of the deacon in regard to the Blood of the Lord.

This ministry is described in the smallest details and there is little to add. At most, we might counsel the deacon to a great freedom in his manner of presenting the chalice. Clearly, he should hold it firmly to avoid any accident, but he should also leave to the communicant the possibility of holding the cup with both hands to approach it to his lips.

The concelebrating priests receive Communion in silence, no doubt because it is supposed that they have said mentally the prayer which the principal celebrant said silently : *Sanguis Domini nostri Iesu Christi.* In the fourth century, the deacon said to all the communicants without exception the formula : *The Blood of Christ, the cup of life.* [40]

The deacon receives Communion last. He does so at the altar. Then he carries the chalice to the credence table where he takes the ablutions. This innovation, taken from the Oriental Liturgies, is a good one. Perhaps, someday, it will be extended to all Masses. At a time when celebration facing the people is spreading everywhere, it is unpleasant to have to take the ablutions at the altar and to cleanse the sacred vessels in the sight of the assembly. It would be more discreet to accomplish these material actions at the credence table or after the Mass. The Ritual of concelebration gives reasonable hope of an evolution of the rite in this direction.

In the list of objects to be prepared for concelebration there is mention of a possible second chalice. Despite the importance of the symbolism of one chalice, the number of concelebrants can, in fact, render necessary the use of a second chalice. But the Ritual makes no allusion to the manner in which this is to be presented to the communicants. True, one of the concelebrants could take it and accomplish a ministry identical to that of the deacon. But there is no reason for not confiding it to a second deacon, either one of the assisting deacons or another deacon who would come to the altar at the

---

[40] *Apostolic Constitutions*, VIII, c. 13, 15, ed. F. X. Funk, *op. cit.*, I, p. 518.

time of Communion. Certain rubricists may object that the assisting deacons do not wear a stole, but this insignia is not indispensable.

When they have received Communion, the concelebrants who are not designated for the distribution of Communion to the faithful go to wash their hands at the credence table and then gain the places they occupied at the beginning of the Mass. Rather than oblige them to go to the credence table, it may often be preferable that one or two clerics present to them a vessel with water and hand towel along the way they take to go from the altar to their places.

The concelebrants remain at their places until the end of Mass.

53. If the number of concelebrants is great, the Bishop principal celebrant or one of the concelebrants, assisted by the deacon, can carry the chalice to each of the concelebrants remaining at their places; these, standing, take the chalice in their hands, drink a little of the consecrated wine, and then return the chalice to him who presented it to them. The deacon wipes the exterior of the chalice.

Nothing prevents the Bishop principal celebrant from presenting the chalice to the first concelebrant, who drinks a little of the consecrated wine, then hands it to the next concelebrant, and so on until the last.

Commentary

As for the Communion of the Body of Christ, the Ritual contains a certain diversity in the ways of Communion with the chalice, so that the rite can be adapted to all situations, especially " if the number of concelebrants is great. "

The first way consists in presenting the chalice to each of the concelebrants, without these displacing themselves : the Bishop, assisted by the deacon, offers the chalice by passing from one to the other. One regrets that, in this way of Communion, the deacon is no longer the principal minister of the chalice, but only the assistant of the

Bishop. It is he nevertheless who presents the chalice to the ministers.

The Bishop can, also, as in the Communion of the Body of Christ, pass the chalice from hand to hand among the concelebrants. It is evident that in such a case, the deacon does not need to intervene : he will receive the chalice when the last of the concelebrants has finished, so that he can present it to the sacred ministers and receive of it himself.

Finally, there exists a third form for Communion with the chalice : each of the concelebrants, having received the Body of Christ over the altar, may likewise receive from the chalice (RC 56).

2. *Communion from the Chalice with a Straw*

54. If Communion from the chalice is to be taken with a straw, one proceeds in the following manner : the Bishop principal celebrant says silently the Quid retribuam Domino... and then receives the straw from the deacon; then he says silently the Sanguis Domini nostri, draws a little of the consecrated wine and then immediately purifies the straw by taking a little water from a vessel placed on the altar near the chalice beforehand by the subdeacon.

Then the deacon places the chalice in the best possible position at the center of the altar, or at the right on a second corporal, i.e., in a place where he himself can most conveniently accomplish his service in the Communion with the chalice. Also near this chalice is placed a vessel with water for cleansing the straw, and a platter on which the straws can be placed after use.

The concelebrants come forward one after the other, and, without genuflecting, receive the straw from the acolyte, and draw forth a little of the consecrated wine; then they purify the straw by taking a little water, and place the straw on the plate that has been placed nearby.

Finally the assisting deacons and the subdeacon come forward to receive the consecrated wine in the same manner; and to the deacon who says to them Sanguis Christi they answer Amen. Then the deacon himself receives and consumes all the consecrated wine remaining, transports the chalice to the nearby table where he purifies it; and the subdeacon wipes and arranges the chalice as usual.

Commentary

The Communion from the chalice with a straw is traditional in the West (above, p. 50), but it constitutes a first lessening of the sign of the participation of all in the same cup. This practice was introduced out of respect for the Blood of Christ, in the fear of letting some drops fall. Today it is a concern with hygiene which has made hopeful its extension outside the papal Mass for those who do not like the idea of drinking out of one cup. It does not seem that it will enjoy a great success.

The Ritual recommends that the deacon place the chalice at a spot where he can " most conveniently accomplish his service. " It is difficult to see in what this service consists in regard to the concelebrants, because these receive in silence. In the Communion of the sacred ministers, the function of the deacon consists in saying to each *Sanguis Christi.* Evidently, his essential task is to watch that all go well in conformity with the prescriptions of the present article.

3.   *Communion from the Chalice with a Spoon*

55. If Communion from the chalice is performed with a spoon, one proceeds in the same manner as in Communion with a straw. The spoon, however, should be placed after Communion in a vessel containing water. The subdeacon, once the Communion is finished, takes the vessel with the spoons in it to a nearby table where he purifies and wipes the spoons.

Commentary

In certain Oriental rites the spoon is used for Communion by intinction : the celebrant takes with the spoon the bread dipped in the chalice, in order to place it in the mouth of the communicant. In the practice which the Ritual of concelebration speaks of, the spoon is used in place of the straw by him who receives. It is in this way that concelebrants receive Communion at a papal Mass. It seems that this way of receiving Communion has its difficulties. The concelebrants must take care to receive Communion directly over the chalice.

Communion of the Body of the Lord Followed Immediately by Communion of the Blood of the Lord

56. Communion of concelebrants may also be carried out in such a way that each concelebrant receive at the altar the Lord's Body and immediately afterwards the Precious Blood.

In this case, the Bishop principal celebrant receives Communion under both species as when he celebrates Mass by himself, while observing in each case the rite chosen for reception of Communion with the chalice, a rite to which the other concelebrants will conform themselves.

After the Communion of the Bishop principal celebrant, the deacon carries the chalice to a second corporal on the right side of the altar, and he remains there to accomplish his service regarding the chalice.

The concelebrants come one by one to the center of the altar, genuflect, and receive the Body of the Lord; then they go to the right side of the altar and receive the Blood of the Lord, according to the rite chosen for Communion with the chalice, as described above.

The Communion of the ministers and the purification of the chalice are carried out in the manner stated above.

Commentary

Before going on to the description of Communion by intinction, the Ritual sets down how each of the concelebrants may receive Communion with the chalice immediately after having received the Body of Christ. This article was already evoked when there was question of the distribution of the consecrated bread (p. 123) and Communion with the chalice (p. 130 f.).

4. *Communion by Intinction*

57. If Communion of the concelebrants is performed by dipping the particles in the Precious Blood, the Bishop principal celebrant receives the Body and Blood of Christ in the usual way, taking care that enough of the consecrated wine remain in the chalice for the Communion of the concelebrants. The deacon then places in the best position possible the chalice either at the center of the altar or at the right on a second corporal, along with the paten containing the particles, in such a place that he himself can the most conveniently assist with the chalice. The concelebrants, one by one, come to the altar, genuflect, take a particle, dip it partially in the chalice, and placing the paten under their mouth, they receive; then, after having washed their hands as described above, they return to the places they had at the beginning of the Mass. Nothing, however, prevents the Bishop principal celebrant himself from giving Communion to the other concelebrants in the following way : after having taken as usual the Body and Blood of the Lord, he gives the chalice and purificator to the deacon; he himself takes the paten or the ciborium with the hosts and, with the deacon at his left, he stands in a place where he can most conveniently give Communion to the concelebrants. The concelebrants, one by one, approach the Bishop principal celebrant, take the paten and stand before the Bishop who dips a part of the host in the chalice and gives it to the communicant, saying nothing. Each communicant, after having received, hands the paten to the next one coming to receive, and then takes his place as at the beginning of the Mass.

The assisting deacons, the deacon and the subdeacon receive Communion in the same way as the concelebrants, but when the Bishop principal celebrant say to them Corpus et Sanguis Christi they respond Amen. The deacon, however, consumes at the altar all the remaining consecrated wine and then carries the chalice to a nearby table where he purifies the chalice; the subdeacon wipes and arranges it as usual.

Commentary

If the concelebrants are going to receive Communion by intinction, the principal celebrant receives first under both species separately as usual. The Ritual reminds him to watch that " there remain enough consecrated wine in the chalice for the Communion of the concelebrants. " The recommendation is a good one, not only in the case of Communion by intinction : the concelebrants first to receive Communion must always take care to leave enough of the wine for those who come after them.

The Communion of the concelebrants by intinction can be done in two ways. The first, which is authorized in all circumstances, consists in the fact that the *concelebrants give themselves Communion* by approaching the altar one by one. One cannot make use of the second form except when the concelebration is presided over by a Bishop : *he gives Communion to the priests.* In the two cases, the communicants must hold in their hand a paten so that no drop of the consecrated wine fall on the corporal.

Though the Ritual does not say so explicitly, it is clear that the deacons and the subdeacon may never give themselves Communion. Therefore, they receive the Eucharist from the hand of the principal celebrant, holding the paten under the mouth (DC 6). When the concelebrating priests have received Communion in silence, the celebrant says to the ministers *Corpus et Sanguis Christi* and they answer, *Amen.*

The deacon, who has received Communion by intinction, then consumes " at the altar all the consecrated wine that remains. " If particles of the bread remain, they are distributed to the faithful.

Communion of the Faithful

58. After the Communion of the concelebrants and the ministers, the Bishop principal celebrant, helped by the deacon of the Mass, says as usual the Ecce Agnus Dei **and the faithful say three times the** Domine non sum dignus. **Then, both he and some of the concelebrants distribute Communion to the faithful, while the Communion antiphon with its psalm is sung.**

If, however, the number of concelebrants is great, the Bishop principal celebrant, after his Communion with the chalice, may immediately distribute Communion to the faithful, while the other concelebrants come forward to receive Communion with the chalice, and afterwards, some of them may help the Bishop in distributing Communion to the faithful. In this case, the Bishop principal celebrant, before the concelebrants receive the Body of the Lord, takes a particle, and holding it for the faithful to see, says Ecce Agnus Dei and then together with the concelebrants and the faithful, he says aloud three times the Domine non sum dignus.

Commentary

After having discussed the Communion of the concelebrants and the sacred ministers, the Ritual goes on immediately to the Communion of the faithful. It would, however, be fitting to foresee beforehand the Communion of priests who did not concelebrate, of the clergy and religious. " In the judgment of the Bishop, " Communion under both species may be given " to the priests who assist at great celebrations and who cannot celebrate or concelebrate, and to lay brothers who assist at concelebration in religious houses " (DC 1).

After this, there is the Communion of the faithful. There is no need for a particular commentary, since the second paragraph of this article has already been discussed above (p. 123).

59.   After the Communion of the faithful, any remaining hosts are consumed by one of the concelebrants, or are carried to the altar of the Blessed Sacrament by a deacon or priest. The Bishop principal celebrant, after having said silently the Quod ore sumpsimus and the Corpus tuum, washes his hands as usual.

Commentary

The Bishop does not take the ablutions, for these are taken by the deacon who purifies the chalice; but he does say the *Quod ore sumpsimus* and the *Corpus tuum*. These two prayers of themselves have nothing to do with the ablutions. They are two Postcommunions, the first being taken from the Mass of Thursday of Passion. The Bishop then washes his hands " as usual, " that is, conforming to the Ceremonial (CE lib. 2, cap. 8, 76).

Conclusion of the Mass

60. After having washed his hands, the Bishop principal celebrant sings the Dominus vobiscum and the Postcommunion, and continues with the conclusion of the Mass.

After he has given the Blessing, all return in procession to the sacristy.

Commentary

Some would like to have all the concelebrants bless the people at the end of the Mass. But such a practice would be contrary to liturgical tradition, which has always given importance to the properly hierarchical character of the action of blessing. It belongs, then, to the president of the assembly to dismiss the people with a blessing : it is by the ministry of the deacon that he gives the order for dismissal; but the blessing which accompanies this dismissal can only come from him.

Rite of the Solemn Mass

1. PREPARATION

61. The concelebrants put on in the sacristy the liturgical vestments which they habitually wear when celebrating Mass alone. The deacon, subdeacon, and the other ministers and servers also vest as usual in the sacristy.

2. THE LITURGY OF THE WORD

Beginning of Mass

62. When all has been prepared, the procession goes through the church to the altar, while the entrance antiphon and its psalm is sung. The concelebrating priests go before the principal celebrant, who is with the deacon and subdeacon.

63. When they have arrived at the altar, the concelebrants, having made the required reverence, ascend the altar two by two and kiss it; then they take the places assigned to them.

64. The principal celebrant, having made his reverence to the altar, says in a subdued voice together with his ministers the prayers to be said at the foot of the altar; then the Mass continues as usual, observing however all that follows.

65. After the incensation of the altar, the principal celebrant goes with the deacon and subdeacon to the seat, and there, after the Kyrie and the Gloria have been sung, he sings the oration.

The Readings

66. Seated, all listen to the Epistle and the chants which follow it.

67. If there are other readings before the Epistle, the lector, once the oration is finished, having made, when required, the proper reverences to the altar and the principal celebrant, goes to the ambo or other suitable place, and there, facing the people, he sings or recites the reading. If there are many readings, they are sung or read in the same way; the principal celebrant, however, says the orations between them, staying at his place, and, genuflecting there at the Flectamus genua, if it occurs.

68. For reading the Epistle, the subdeacon, once the oration is finished, takes the book and, after having made, if need be, the required reverences to the altar and to the principal celebrant, he goes to the ambo or other suitable place, and there, facing the people, sings or reads the Epistle. Afterwards he goes to the principal celebrant and receives his blessing.

69. After blessing the subdeacon, the principal celebrant, seated, places and blesses the incense. Then the deacon takes the Book of the Gospels to the altar and places it in the middle, and, kneeling, he says the Munda cor meum; he takes the book from the altar, goes to the principal celebrant who is standing, and asks his blessing; then, accompanied by the thurifer, acolytes and subdeacon, he goes to the ambo or other suitable place, and there, facing the people, sings or reads the Gospel.

70. If there is to be a homily, it is given by the principal celebrant or by one of the concelebrants; after it, the principal celebrant, at his place, begins the Credo, if there is to be one.

71. After the Creed, the principal celebrant says Dominus vobiscum and Oremus, and the Prayer of the Faithful takes place, according to custom.

3. *THE EUCHARISTIC LITURGY*

Offertory

72. When the Offertory antiphon is begun, the ministers bring the offerings to the altar, and all is carried out as usual for the Offertory. Then the principal celebrant, together with the other concelebrants, goes to the altar and makes the required reverence, and then with the deacon he goes up to the altar and kisses it. The other concele-

brants, however, having made the required reverence
stand on the floor around the altar, but in such a way as not
to interfere with the Offertory rite. If it seems fitting, the
concelebrants may come to the altar just before the principal celebrant sings the Prayer over the Gifts.

73. At the Offertory, all is carried out as described above
in numbers 30-34, omitting, however, what is proper to the
Pontifical Mass.

Canon

74. In the Canon also, everything is to be observed as
stated in numbers 35-42.

Communion

75. Both in the preparation for Communion and at the
Communion of the concelebrants, ministers and faithful,
all is to be observed as stated above in numbers 43-58,
excluding however what is proper to a Pontifical Mass.

The deacon receives the kiss of peace after the concelebrants and gives it to the subdeacon, who brings it, in the
usual way, to the clergy.

Conclusion of the Mass

76. After the Communion of the faithful or the Communion
with the chalice, each concelebrant washes his hands and
returns to the place he had at the beginning of Mass.
The principal celebrant, after washing his hands, says
Dominus vobiscum and the Postcommunion, and continues
with the conclusion of the Mass.

After the Blessing, all return in procession to the sacristy.

Commentary

In the Ritual of concelebration, it is the solemn Mass
of the Bishop surrounded by his *presbyterium*, ministers,
and all the people of God which presents itself as " the
principal manifestation of the Church " according to the

teaching of the Council (C 41). Far from giving the impression that the solemn Mass and the sung Mass are the " making-solemn " of a recited Mass, the Ritual shows them as simplified forms of the Pontifical Mass, conforming to the liturgical tradition anterior to the Missal of St. Pius V. That is the reason why it begins with a detailed description of a concelebration presided over by the Bishop. To the entire description of the solemn Mass, the following statement, often repeated, can be applied : one will observe all that is found above, " excluding the rites proper to the Pontifical Mass " (RC 75).

A certain number of articles, such as those which deal with the Liturgy of the Word, may seem superfluous since they only repeat the *Ritus servandus in celebratione missae*, promulgated on January 27, 1965. The reason is that the text of the Ritual of concelebration was prepared prior to the Ritual of celebration. In the concelebrations which were authorized *ad experimentum* from the summer of 1964, one already celebrated the Liturgy of the Word away from the altar, even though the *Ritus servandus* of the Mass had not yet been revised.

There is practically no commentary to offer for the rites of the solemn Mass, the sung Mass, and the recited Mass. Celebrants should conform to the rules of the new rites of the Mass and those rules decreed for the concelebrated Pontifical Mass.

However, two brief comments are in order. The first concerns the Offertory : in the solemn Mass (RC 72), the offering of the gifts by the faithful, mentioned in the Pontifical Mass (RC 29), has been forgotten. The second point refers to the kiss of peace : if it is specified that the deacon and subdeacon receive the kiss of peace after the concelebrants (RC 75), this is because at a Pontifical Mass the Bishop gives it to them at the moment of their Communion (RC 50).

Rite of the Mass with a Deacon

77. All those things that pertain to the principal celebrant, the concelebrants, deacon and ministers or servers are done as stated above for a solemn Mass. Besides, this form of Mass must be considered as a solemn Mass.

78. The Epistle is sung or read by a lector or capable server, or, if there is none, then by the deacon himself.

Commentary

The rules concerning a Mass with a deacon are found in the Ritual for the Celebration of Mass under chapter XIV (RS 95-98). We should remember that the Bishop can concelebrate with only one deacon as a sacred minister (I 47).

Since there is question here of a form of the solemn Mass (RC 77), the deacon may, with the permission of the Bishop, receive Communion under both species (DC 1). [41]

---

[41] The Ordinances of the French Bishops are all in agreement on this authorization.

Rite of the Sung Mass

1.   *PREPARATION*

79.   The concelebrants vest in the sacristy in the vestments which they habitually wear for celebrating Mass alone.

The ministers or servers also put on their proper vestments.

2.   *THE LITURGY OF THE WORD*

Beginning of Mass

80.   When all has been prepared, the procession goes through the church to the altar, while the entrance antiphon and its psalm is sung.   The concelebrating priests walk before the principal celebrant.

81.   When they have arrived at the altar, the concelebrants, having made the required reverence, ascend the altar two by two and kiss it; then they take the places assigned to them.

82.   The principal celebrant, after having made his reverence to the altar, says in a subdued voice together with his ministers the prayers at the foot of the altar; then the Mass continues as usual, observing however all that follows.

83.   After kissing the altar, or if he uses incense, after the incensation of the altar, the principal celebrant goes to his seat and there, after the Kyrie and the Gloria have been sung, he sings the oration.

The Readings

84.   Seated, all listen to the Epistle and the chants which follow it.

85.   The readings and the Epistle are proclaimed by a lector or a capable server who, having made, when required,

the proper reverences to the altar and the principal celebrant, goes to the ambo or other suitable place and there, facing the people, reads or sings the reading or the Epistle. If there are many readings, they are sung or read in the same way; the principal celebrant, at his place, says the orations between the readings, and makes the genuflection there for the Flectamus genua, if it occurs.

If there is no lector, the readings and the Epistle are proclaimed, in the same manner as already described, by one of the concelebrants.

86.   The Gospel may be sung or read by a deacon who, towards the end of the chants which follow the Epistle, carries the Book of the Gospels to the altar, places it in the center and, kneeling, says the Munda cor meum; then he rises, takes the book from the altar, goes to the principal celebrant to receive his blessing; finally, he goes to the ambo or other suitable place, and there, facing the people, he sings or reads the Gospel. When he has finished, he brings the Book of the Gospels to the principal celebrant who kisses it.

If there is no deacon, one of the concelebrants sings or reads the Gospel; bowing profoundly, he says the Munda cor meum, but he does not ask for the blessing.

87.   If there is a homily, it is given by the principal celebrant or one of the concelebrants; when he has finished, the principal celebrant, at his place, begins the Credo, if there is to be one.

88.   After the Creed, the principal celebrant says Dominus vobiscum and Oremus, and the Prayer of the Faithful follows, according to the custom of the place.

3.   *THE EUCHARISTIC LITURGY*

Offertory

89.   When the Offertory antiphon is begun, one of the concelebrants brings the offerings to the altar, and all is carried out as usual for the Offertory. Then the principal celebrant, together with the other concelebrants, goes to the altar and makes the required reverence. After this, he alone ascends the altar and kisses it. The other concele-

brants, having made the required reverence, stand on the
floor around the altar but in such a way as not to interfere
with the Offertory rite. If it seems fitting, the concelebrants may come to the altar just before the principal
celebrant sings the Prayer over the Gifts.

90. At the Offertory, all is carried out as described above
in numbers 30-34, omitting, however, what is proper to the
Pontifical Mass and what should be done by sacred ministers.

Canon

91. In the Canon also, everything is to be observed as
stated in numbers 35-42.

Communion

92. Both in the preparation for Communion and at the
Communion of the concelebrants and the faithful, all
is to be observed as stated above in numbers 43-51, excluding however what is proper to the Pontifical Mass. All
that is proper to the deacon in the Communion rite is
carried out by one of the concelebrants.

Conclusion of the Mass

93. After the Communion of the faithful or the Communion
with the chalice, each concelebrant washes his hands and
returns to the place he had at the beginning of the Mass.
The principal celebrant, after washing his hands, says
Dominus vobiscum and the Postcommunion, and continues
with the conclusion of the Mass.
After the Blessing, all return in procession to the sacristy.

Commentary

The legislator, as can easily be seen, has taken care to
respect the diversity of ministers in all the various forms
of the concelebrated Mass. In the sung Mass (RC 85-86),
as also in the recited Mass (RC 100-101), the readings

should be carried out by the appropriate minister, lector or deacon. It is only in their absence that one of the concelebrating priests will substitute and fulfill their ministry.

A question arises as to what is the difference between the Mass with a deacon and a sung Mass at which a deacon reads or sings the Gospel (RC 86). In the first case, the deacon, normally vested in dalmatic, fulfills all the deacon's functions in relation to the celebrant, from the beginning of the Mass to the *Ite, missa est* at the end. In the second case, the deacon intervenes only for the proclamation of the Gospel. During the rest of the Mass, he can fulfill other functions, such as directing the singing of the people. When he reads the Gospel, he should, nevertheless, be vested in alb and stole (RS 44). He will not be able to receive Communion from the chalice, since this faculty is given only to the sacred ministers of a solemn Mass (DC 1).

When the Gospel is proclaimed by one of the concelebrants, he does not ask a blessing from the principal celebrant but, at the end of the reading, he brings the book to him to be kissed, as the Ritual explicitly states (RC 86).

Rite of Recited Mass

1. *PREPARATION*

94. The concelebrants vest in the sacristy in the vestments they habitually wear for celebrating Mass alone.

The servers also put on their proper vestments.

Commentary

The majority of the rules for a recited Mass when it is concelebrated have been inserted in the *Ritus servandus in celebratione Missae* and in the Ordinary of the Mass. Thus, they no longer manifest a character proper to concelebration. For this reason, there will be hereafter no change in the celebration of the Liturgy of the Word away from the altar and in the possibility of the concelebrants singing with the people or reciting together the Proper and the Ordinary.

Some points, however, should hold our attention, since they allow us to understand the concelebration rite better.

2. *THE LITURGY OF THE WORD*

Beginning of Mass

95. When all has been prepared, the concelebrants, preceded by the servers, go to the altar, all with hands folded. The principal celebrant walks last.

96. When they arrive at the altar, the concelebrants, having made the required reverence, ascend the altar two by two and kiss it; then they take the places assigned to them.

97. The prayers at the foot of the altar are said as usual by the principal celebrant alone with the server, while a popular hymn is sung. If, however, there is no hymn,

these prayers may be said by the principal celebrant alternating with all those present.

Commentary

This article clearly formulates the respective importance of the prayers at the foot of the altar and that of the entrance hymn.   It is more important to have this popular hymn during the entrance rite than to offer to the faithful the possibility of dialoguing the preparatory prayers with the priest.   Only when this hymn is absent may the prayers be said alternately between the principal celebrant and all present.   The rule is excellent : it comes from the very structure of the entrance liturgy.

98.   It is fitting that the principal celebrant and the concelebrants recite or sing together with the people, if they are present, the Ordinary of the Mass which pertains to the congregation.   Moreover, nothing prevents the concelebrants from saying also, in the absence of those to whom it pertains to say them, the Introit and Offertory antiphons with their psalms and the chants between the readings.

Commentary

The concelebrants may sing with the people " if they are present " *(si adest)*.   This short, incidental remark reveals the mind of the legislator on an important point : concelebration is not reserved to exceptional circumstances.   In the absence of the assembly, concelebration manifests better the unity of the priesthood than a multiplicity of individual Masses, which, with or without an indult, were often solitary Masses.

The Readings

99.   All, seated, listen to the Epistle and the chants that follow.

100.   The readings and the Epistle are proclaimed by a lector or a capable server who, having made, when required,

the proper reverences to the altar and the principal cele-brant, goes to the ambo or other suitable place, and there, facing the people, recites the reading or the Epistle.

If there are many readings, they are read according to the same ceremony; the principal celebrant at his place says the orations between the Readings and make the genuflection there at the Flectamus genua, if it occurs.

If there is no lector, the readings and the Epistle are proclaimed, in the same manner as stated above, by one of the concelebrants.

101.   The Gospel may be read by a deacon who, toward the end of the chants which follow the Epistle, carries the Book of the Gospels to the altar and places it in the center; kneeling, he says the Munda cor meum; then he takes the book from the altar, goes to the principal celebrant to receive his blessing; he goes to the ambo or another suitable place and there, facing the people, he reads the Gospel.   At the conclusion, he brings the book to the principal celebrant who kisses it.

If there is no deacon, one of the concelebrants reads the Gospel; bowing profoundly, he says the Munda cor meum, but he does not ask for the blessing.

102.   If there is to be a homily, it is given by the principal celebrant or by one of the concelebrants; when it is finished, the principal celebrant, at his place, begins the Credo, if there is to be one.

103.   After the Creed, the principal celebrant says Dominus vobiscum and Oremus, and the Prayer of the Faithful follows, according to the custom of the place.

3.   *THE EUCHARISTIC LITURGY*

Offertory

104.   When the Offertory antiphon has been recited, one of the concelebrants carries the offerings to the altar and all is performed as usual for the Offertory.   The principal celebrant together with the concelebrants goes to the altar and, after having made the required reverence, all take their places around the altar.   Only the principal celebrant kisses the altar.

Commentary

A difference is to be noted between the recited Mass and
the various forms of the sung Mass. At the sung Masses,
whether Mass of a Bishop, solemn Mass or sung Mass
without ministers, the concelebrants leave their places
and " stand on the floor around the altar but in such
a way as not to interfere with the Offertory rites " (RC 29,
72, 89). They approach the altar only for the Prayer over
the Gifts (RC 32), unless it seems convenient to do this
earlier (RC 72, 89). At the recited Mass, the intermediate
position between their original place and the altar does
not exist; the concelebrants, therefore, from the beginning
of the Offertory, take the place they will have during
the Canon.

105. At the Offertory, all is carried out as stated above in
numbers 30-34, excluding what is proper to a Pontifical
Mass or to a sung Mass.

Canon

106. For the Canon, all is to be observed as stated above in
numbers 35-42.

Communion

107. Both in the preparation for Communion and at the
Communion of the concelebrants and the faithful, all
is to be observed as stated above in numbers 43-58, excluding however what is proper to a Pontifical Mass or to a sung
Mass. The kiss of peace may be given to the concelebrants. All that is proper to the deacon in the Communion
rite is carried out by one of the concelebrants.

Commentary

" All that is proper to the deacon in the Communion rite
is carried out by one of the concelebrants. " It is still
necessary to admit that, if a deacon is present, he can

perform at the recited Mass all the deacon's functions without limiting himself to the proclamation of the Gospel. The Mass with a deacon is, by its very nature, a solemn Mass (RS 95, RC 77) but a larger interpretation has quickly prevailed. This comes from the practice of the Council itself: during the fourth session of the Council, all the Masses were celebrated with a deacon or, in the absence of a deacon during the school vacations, with the assistance of a priest vested in alb and wearing the stole in the priestly manner.

When Bishops and priests concelebrate without the assistance of a deacon, the deacon's functions are not to be performed by one of the concelebrating Bishops; it is a priest who will read the Gospel and the intentions of the Prayer of the Faithful; but it is fitting that one of the Bishops give the homily.

Conclusion of the Mass

108. After the Communion of the faithful or the Communion with the chalice, each concelebrant washes his hands and returns to the place he had at the beginning of the Mass. The principal celebrant, after having washed his hands, says Dominus vobiscum and the Postcommunion, and continues with the conclusion of the Mass.

After the Blessing, all return to the sacristy.

Concelebration of Mass in which Ordination to the Priesthood is Conferred

The Ritual of concelebration deals with the Ordination of priests before speaking of episcopal Consecration because it is following the order of the Roman Pontifical. The Pontifical gives the Ordination rites in ascending order : it begins with Tonsure and ends with episcopal Consecration; afterwards, it gives the rites of the blessing of persons reserved to the Bishop and the first of these blessings is that of an Abbot.

109. The Mass in which priestly Ordination is conferred is organized according to the rite given above for concelebration. If, besides the priesthood, the subdiaconate and the diaconate are also conferred at this Mass, one of those ordained in this same liturgical action takes on the function of deacon and another that of subdeacon, from the time he receives the Order. Consequently, at the beginning of the Mass, these functions are performed by a deacon and subdeacon previously ordained.

Commentary

It should not be necessary to specify that the deacon and subdeacon who assisted the Bishop during the first part of the Mass should not now return to the sacristy and take off their vestments, after having given their place of serving the Bishop to the newly ordained ministers. Rather, they keep their place in the sanctuary and are allowed to receive Communion under both species. The multiplicity of deacons and subdeacons around the *presbyterium* will thus manifest the diversity of orders and of ministers in the liturgical assembly.

110. Those who are to be ordained priests enter the church together with the others in the usual manner and take the places assigned to them in the choir, in the sanctuary, or in some other place deemed suitable.

111. The Ordination takes place in the usual way, as described in the Pontifical, with the exceptions which follow.

112. The priests whom the Bishop allow to concelebrate with the newly ordained priests are the first, after the Bishop, to impose hands on the heads of the new priests.

113. A chasuble that is not folded or pinned up on either side is put on each of the new priests.

Commentary

The custom of vesting the newly ordained priests in a chasuble folded up on the shoulders goes back to Durand de Mende. [42] How was such an aberration able to last for nearly seven centuries? And how could serious commentators try to give it a mystical interpretation?

As for the vesting ceremony, mention should be made of an indult obtained by the Cardinal-Archbishop of Milan (March 10, 1965) : the Archbishop may be assisted by his auxiliaries in the placing of the sacred vestments on the subdeacons, deacons and priests; the Archbishop places the vestment saying the formula in the plural, while the auxiliary Bishops, vested in stole, cope and miter, carry out the same rite but in silence. [43]

114. While the Offertory antiphon with its psalm is being sung or recited, the Bishop with miter on sits at his throne or faldstool and receives the offerings from all the newly ordained; then, he washes his hands, rises, and proceeds to the altar as usual to continue the Mass.

Commentary

According to ancient Roman usage, it is at his throne that the Bishop should confer ordinations : *Stat pontifex*

---

[42] M. Andrieu, op. cit., III : " Le Pontifical de Guillaume Durand, " p. 368.

[43] *Notitiae*, art. cit., p. 159.

in sede sua, singillatim imponens manus capitibus eorum et benedicet eos. [44]   There was still witness to this in the thirteenth century in the Pontifical of the Curia. [45]   But the diffusion of the Pontifical of William Durand soon made widespread the practice of ordinations at the altar, [46] a practice preserved until now.   In authorizing the Bishop to receive the offerings of the new priests at his throne, the Ritual of concelebration is returning again to traditional practice.

115.   When the newly ordained have finished offering their gifts, the concelebrating priests go to the altar, and the Mass continues in the manner stated above for each form of concelebration.

Commentary

The present Ritual abolishes, without need of further decrees, all the rubrics of the Pontifical which treat of the concelebration of new priests : " The Mass continues in the manner stated above for each form of concelebration. " It is greatly desired that only one form be retained, namely the most noble form (C 113), the solemn liturgy.

The newly ordained priests should have the place of honor in this first Mass that they concelebrate.   It is fitting, therefore, that they be the closest to the Bishop around the altar.

116.   After giving the kiss of peace to the newly ordained priests, the Bishop gives it to the assistant priest, and, if there are any, to the other concelebrants, then to the assisting deacons, and also to one of those ordained to each sacred Order : each comes to the Bishop one after the other, gives in turn the kiss of peace to the next one of his Order, and he to the next, until the last one receives it.

---

[44] Ordo Romanus 36, 18 in M. Andrieu, *op. cit.*, IV, p. 198.

[45] M. Andrieu, *op. cit.*, II : " Le Pontifical de la Curie Romaine au 13e siècle, " X, 33-34, p. 349.

[46] M. Andrieu, *op. cit.*, III : " Le Pontifical de Guillaume Durand, " lib. 1, XI, 9, p. 354.

If those ordained are small in number, the Bishop may give the kiss of peace to each individual.

117. Communion of all the concelebrants takes place in the manner indicated in the rite for concelebration; during this time, the responsory Iam non dicam is sung.

Commentary

Hereafter, at the Ordination Mass, there are two chants for the Communion : the responsory *Iam non dicam* which accompanies the Communion of the concelebrants, and the Communion antiphon with its psalm which accompanies the Communion of the clergy and the people (RC 118). Until now, the responsory *Iam non dicam* was sung after Communion according to the rule introduced by Durand de Mende. [47]

118. If Communion under both species is to be distributed to those newly ordained, it is to be done after the Communion of the concelebrants is finished, with the observance of the Communion rite given below. Meanwhile, some of the newly ordained priests distribute Communion to the faithful. During this time, the Communion antiphon with its psalm is sung.

Commentary

If there are many ordained, it will be necessary to have at least two chalices. The new deacons will be the ones to present the chalices to the communicants. It would also be fitting that some of the newly ordained deacons distribute Communion along with the newly ordained priests, since, according to the words of the constitution *Lumen Gentium* (n. 29), they are henceforth ordinary ministers of the Eucharist.

119. After the Communion, the newly ordained priests take places in front of the altar, before the Bishop, and make their profession of faith. The Bishop sitting at the

---

[47] *Ibid.*, lib. i, XIII, 23, p. 371.

faldstool before the center of the altar, places his hands on the head of each of the ordained and says : Accipe Spiritum Sanctum; omitting the formula Stola innocentiae induat te Dominus he receives the promise of fidelity from each of those ordained; finally, he admonishes and blesses them. After this, the newly ordained priests return to the places they had at the beginning of the Mass.

Commentary

The only innovations introduced by this article are the following : after having received Communion, the newly ordained concelebrants do not immediately take the places they had during the Liturgy of the Word, but they stand before the altar for the concluding rites. These latter rites no longer include the letting down of the chasuble with the accompanying formula *Stola innocentiae.* After the blessing *ut sitis benedicti in ordine sacerdotali* which is only for the new priests, these now join the other concelebrants in the *presbyterium*.

120. The Bishop rises, kisses the altar, says Dominus vobiscum and the Postcommunion and continues the Mass as usual.

121. After the Bishop has said the Placeat and before he gives the blessing, he sits at the faldstool at the center of the altar and gives the allocution to those ordained; then he rises, gives the solemn blessing, and all return in procession to the sacristy.

Commentary

The final admonition which, since the fifteenth century, the Bishop addresses to all those ordained, takes place, according to the Pontifical, between the blessing of the people and the Last Gospel. Now, since the Last Gospel has been suppressed, this admonition has been inserted curiously enough between the prayer *Placeat* and the last blessing. It might have been better to suppress it without further ado or, at least, put it before the dismissal of the assembly.

Concelebration of Mass in which Episcopal Consecration is Conferred

122. The Mass in which episcopal Consecration is conferred is conducted according to the rite for concelebration given above with the following exceptions.

Commentary

The Ritual of concelebration abolishes, without need of further decrees, all the rubrics of the Roman Pontifical which treat of the concelebration at the Mass of an episcopal Consecration. Since it was necessary to adapt the rites of Consecration to the new Ordo of Consecration, the occasion was taken to introduce some simplifications without waiting for the complete reform of the first book of the Pontifical.

123. The one to be consecrated stays with the other concelebrants on the way to the altar and in the sanctuary; therefore, no special chapel is to be prepared for him. Furthermore, from the beginning he wears all the liturgical vestments, white in color, which are required for a Pontifical Mass, with the exception of those articles which are to be blessed and given to him during the Consecration itself.

Commentary

At the Mass for Ordination of priests, these latter said all the prayers of the Ordinary together with the Bishop, beginning with the Offertory. But for the Consecration of a Bishop, even more was required of the two concelebrants : the Bishop-elect was to read the entire formulary of the Liturgy of the Word at a small altar erected for this purpose. This was his " private chapel, " which the Ritual declares henceforth abolished.

The private chapel was also used for the double vesting of the new Bishop. He entered the church with rochet and mozzetta; he vested in alb and cope for the first part of the rite (postulation, oath, examination) taking place before the Liturgy of the Word; then he went back to his chapel to receive the stockings and sandals and to put on the chasuble.

This double vesting, which dates back to the twelfth century, [48] is now suppressed; the new Bishop puts on all the liturgical vestments, white in color, in the sacristy. However, he does not receive the staff and ring, nor gloves and miter, since these will be given to him during the Consecration itself.

124. The co-consecrating Bishops, if they are going to concelebrate, also vest at the beginning in the vestments required for concelebration.

Commentary

Up to now, the co-consecrating Bishops put on only the amice and cope over the rochet, and the miter. Now, if they are going to concelebrate — which is eminently suitable, according to RC 5 *(valde convenit)* — they will vest in the liturgical vestments needed for Mass, but will not wear tunic or dalmatic (RC 12).

125. The oath, if it is to be taken then, may be taken at a more convenient time or even in the sacristy immediately before the Consecration itself. In this event, however, the postulation by the first co-consecrating Bishop and the reading of the apostolic mandate are to take place at the beginning of the Consecration, before the examination of the one to be consecrated.

---

[48] M. Andrieu, *op. cit.*, I : " Le Pontifical romain du 12e siècle, " X, 9, p. 141. If the double clothing goes back to the 12th century, the private chapel is not attested to before the 15th century.

Commentary

The taking of an oath by the Bishop-elect was already frequently practiced. Thus this article does not actually innovate.

126. In conferring the Consecration, all things are observed as contained in the Roman Pontifical. **However, the imposition of hands can be done by all Bishops present, vested in choir dress, with the Bishops who are going to concelebrate at the Mass taking precedence over the others. The words** Accipe Spiritum Sanctum **are said only by the consecrating Bishop and the two co-consecrating Bishops.**

Commentary

The Constitution of the Council declares that " in the episcopal Consecration, all the Bishops present may impose hands " (C 76) so as to make evident that the one to be consecrated is entering the episcopal College. The *Inter Oecumenici* instruction regulated this rite as early as 1964 : " At the episcopal Consecration, all the Bishops present, dressed in choir habit, may perform the imposition of hands. Only the Bishop who is consecrator and the two co-consecrating Bishops say the words *Accipe Spiritum Sanctum* " (I 69). The Ritual of concelebration is content with reproducing the words of the instruction, while specifying that the Bishops who are going to concelebrate the Mass perform the imposition of hands immediately after the co-consecrating Bishops.

127. After the Consecration, the new Bishop wipes his head and washes his hands in the sacristy or some other more suitable place.

Commentary

According to the Pontifical, the new Bishop was to wipe his head and wash his hands at his private chapel. Henceforth, he will do this in a more secluded place. But why oblige him to wipe off without delay every external trace of the Consecration he has just received? When costly perfume has been poured on the head of a person we wish to honor, he usually tries to keep it as long as possible! Such kind of rubricism will always remain blind to the language of signs!

128. While the Offertory antiphon with its psalm is being sung, the consecrating Bishop, with miter on, sits at the throne or faldstool and receives the offering of the newly consecrated Bishop; then he washes his hands, rises, and proceeds to the altar as usual.

Commentary

See the commentary on article 114.

129. After the newly consecrated Bishop's offering has been presented, the Mass continues according to the form for concelebration given above.

Commentary

See the commentary on article 115.

130. The Prayer over the Gifts, added to the Prayer of the Mass, is said by the consecrating Bishop alone. In the Canon, however, only the newly consecrated Bishop says the Hanc igitur.

Commentary

According to the Pontifical, the consecrating Bishop and the new Bishop together said the Prayer over the Gifts and the *Hanc igitur*. Henceforth, these two formularies are divided between the two. The *Hanc igitur* of the Mass of Consecration of a Bishop goes back to at least the sixth century, for it is found in the Sacramentary of Verona. [49]

---

[49] *Sacramentarium Veronense*, ed. Mohlberg (Rome 1955), n° 944.

Until the thirteenth century, it was said by the consecrator alone; it was Durand de Mende who had the new Bishop also say it. [50]

131. After the Postcommunion, the consecrator blesses and gives the miter and gloves to the newly consecrated Bishop, and he enthrones him; while the hymn Te Deum is being sung, the new Bishop, going through the church, gives his blessing to all, as stated in the Pontifical.

132. At the end of the hymn, the antiphon Firmetur with its versicles and the oration are said; after this, the consecrator says Dominus vobiscum and adds Ite, missa est. Then the newly consecrated Bishop, with miter and staff, goes to the consecrator and sings or says Ad multos annos.

The consecrator and the co-consecrating Bishops receive the new Bishop with the kiss of peace. Finally, the newly consecrated Bishop alone gives the solemn blessing, and all return in procession to the sacristy.

Commentary

In order to understand the modifications which the Ritual of concelebration has introduced into the last part of the episcopal Consecration, it may be helpful to make a comparison between the two practices :

Roman Pontifical	*Ritual of concelebration*
Postcommunion.	Postcommunion.
Ite, missa est.	
Placeat.	
Blessing of the people by the consecrating Bishop.	
Blessing and giving of the miter.	Blessing and giving of the miter.
Blessing and giving of the gloves.	Blessing and giving of the gloves.

---

[50] M. Andrieu, *op. cit.*, III : " Le Pontifical de Guillaume Durand, " lib. I, XIV, 52, p. 388.

Enthroning.	Enthroning.
Te Deum.	*Te Deum.*
Antiphon *Firmetur* and its oration.	Antiphon *Firmetur* and its oration.
	Dismissal of the assembly by the consecrator.
	Ad multos annos.
	Kiss given to the new Bishop by the three consecrators.
Blessing of the people by the new Bishop.	Blessing of the people by the new Bishop.
Ad multos annos.	
Kiss given to the new Bishop by the three consecrators.	

This new organization of the rites contains two innovations : all the concluding rites take place before the dismissal of the assembly and there is only one final blessing, that of the new Bishop.

Concelebration of Mass in which an Abbot is Blessed

133. The Mass in which an Abbot is blessed is conducted according to the rite for concelebration designated above, with the exceptions which follow. The one to be blessed stays with the other concelebrants both on the way to the altar and in the sanctuary; accordingly, it is not necessary to prepare a special chapel. From the beginning, moreover, he wears all the sacred vestments required for a Pontifical Mass, with the exception of those articles to be blessed and presented to him later.

134. The assisting Abbots, if they are going to concelebrate, wear from the beginning the vestments required for concelebration.

135. The oath, if it is to be taken then, may be taken at a more convenient time or even in the sacristy immediately before the Blessing itself. The presentation and examination of the one to be blessed, and, if called for, the reading of the apostolic mandate, are to be done before the litany, omitting psalms and antiphon.

136. The entire rite for the Blessing is carried out as given in the Pontifical.

137. While the antiphon with its psalm is sung or read, the Bishop wearing his miter, sits at the throne or faldstool and receives the offering of the new Abbot; he then washes his hands, rises and proceeds to the altar as usual to continue the Mass, according to the form for concelebration given above.

138. After the Postcommunion, the Bishop blesses the miter and gloves and gives them to the new Abbot, and he places him in the Abbot's throne or the faldstool before the altar. While the hymn Te Deum is being sung, the new Abbot, going through the church, gives to all his blessing.

139. After the hymn, and the verses and oration which follow, the Bishop says Dominus vobiscum and adds Ite, missa est. Then, the new Abbot, with miter and staff, goes to the Bishop and sings or says Ad multos annos. The Bishop and the assisting Abbots receive the new

Abbot with the kiss of peace. Finally, the new Abbot
gives the solemn blessing, and all return in procession
to the sacristy.

Commentary

As can easily be seen, the articles devoted by the Ritual
of concelebration to the Mass in which an Abbot is blessed
are modeled on those which treat of the episcopal Consecration. This is as it should be, for the rites of an abbatial
Blessing are a development of the Consecration of a
Bishop.

The *Ordo de benedictione Abbatis auctoritate Apostolica*
goes back substantially to the Romano-Germanic Pontifical
of the tenth century from which the present Pontifical
takes its form : Litany of the Saints during the prostration
of the Abbot-elect, versicles and orations, preface of the
Blessing, bestowal of the Rule and the cross, the *Te
Deum*. [51]   It is in the Pontifical of the Curia of the
thirteenth century that we find the Abbot described as
wearing the *pontificalia* : stockings, sandals, tunic, dalmatic,
gloves, ring and miter. [52]   Moreover, a special chapel,
removed from the Bishop's throne, is set aside for him,
and it is there that he reads all the texts of the Liturgy
of the Word; but he assists silently at the Eucharist and
he does not receive Communion from the chalice. In the
same epoch, Durand de Mende has the Seven Penitential
Psalms sung before the Litany and decrees that the new

---

[51] C. Vogel, *Le Pontifical romano-germanique du dixième siècle*, XXVI
(Vatican City 1963), pp. 62-69. The critical text, edited by C. Vogel,
has not kept the mention of the giving of the gloves, as did the
edition of Hittorp. One should bear this correction in mind when
reading page 58 of the very interesting study of P. Salmon, *Les
insignes du pontife dans le rite romain* (Rome 1955).

[52] M. Andrieu, *op. cit.*, II : " Le Pontifical de la Curie...," XVI, 1,
p. 409.

Abbot be enthroned in his abbatial chair or in the stall of a cathedral dignitary. [53]

The ceremony of the abbatial Blessing reaches its full development in the Roman Pontifical of 1485 : the special chapel for the Abbot-elect is prepared in the sanctuary, the double vesting is inspired by that found in the episcopal Consecration, the miter and gloves receive a blessing and are given by the Bishop; there is the beginning of a pseudo-concelebration but it lacks the essential of this rite in order to have sacramental value, because the new Abbot does not say the words of Consecration. Besides, he may not receive Communion from the chalice.

Thus we can see that the Ritual of 1965 has modified the Ordo of the Abbatial Blessing : it has simplified it in suppressing the singing of the Seven Penitential Psalms (RC 135); it has placed the Blessing in a true concelebration; it has harmonized the rubrics with those of the episcopal Consecration, especially the complementary rites : they will now take place before the dismissal of the assembly and not after the *Ite, missa est*. The importance of a first blessing is always esteemed, yet some will perhaps be surprised that the blessing of the new Abbot, at the end of the Mass, is substituted for that of the Bishop (RC 139).

---

[53] M. Andrieu, *op. cit.*, III : " Le Pontifical de Guillaume Durand, " lib, I, XX, pp. 400-408.

Rite of Concelebration for Priests who are Infirm

1. *GENERAL NORMS*

140. Priests who are infirm, as long as they are not lying down, may concelebrate Mass with another priest who is not infirm, with the observance either of the rite for concelebration or of the norms which follow.

141. Priests who have poor eyesight, or who are totally blind, may also use this rite.

142. The principal celebrating priest must wear all the sacred vestments as usual. The priests who are infirm, however, are to wear, only in so far as it is possible for them to do so, at least an alb, surplice or choir habit, and a stole.

143. Before the principal celebrant comes to the altar, the priests who are infirm are given positions around the altar, in seats prepared for them, in whatever location most convenient. Those who have permission, moreover, to remain seated throughout the celebration, may also make use of this permission in concelebration.

2. *THE LITURGY OF THE WORD*

144. The principal celebrant performs and says all those things described above for the rite of concelebration.

145. The concelebrants, however, if they can, alternate with the principal celebrant in saying the prayers at the foot of the altar and the Kyrie; and they recite the Gloria and Credo with him. It is sufficient, however, for them to listen to the Introit antiphon and the chants occurring between the readings.

146. In the absence of a qualified minister to proclaim the readings, Epistle and Gospel, one or another of the concelebrants, or the principal celebrant himself, may read them.

3.   *THE EUCHARISTIC LITURGY*

147. After the Offertory antiphon, the concelebrants, if they can, come to the altar before the principal celebrant says the Prayer over the Gifts; they take their places around or near the table of the altar, in the most convenient place.

148. The Offertory prayers are said silently by the principal celebrant alone.

149. The Prayer over the Gifts is said by the principal celebrant alone, to which the others reply Amen.   The Preface, also, is said by the principal celebrant, the others making the responses in the dialogue which precedes it, and saying the Sanctus together with the principal celebrant.

150. The Canon is said as explained above.   All the concelebrants, however, must say together with the principal celebrant all the words from the Hanc igitur to the Supplices inclusive.   Each one makes the gestures as well as he can.

151. The Lord's Prayer is said together by all the concelebrants but the embolism is said by the principal celebrant alone.

152. The principal celebrant gives the kiss of peace to each one of the concelebrants individually, if they cannot give it to one another.

153. The prayers before Communion are said silently by the principal celebrant alone.

154. The rite for Communion is to be chosen from among those described below, according to what is more suitable. The principal celebrant, however, if it seems preferable, may give Communion under both species to each of the concelebrants, after he himself has received Communion under both species.

155. After Communion, the concelebrants return to the places they had at the beginning of the Mass.   The principal celebrant purifies the chalice and carries out the other rubrics as usual for concluding the Mass.

Commentary

A commentary on the rite of concelebration for priests who are infirm cannot be based on any historical evidence. This Ordo constitutes a total innovation and we should welcome it with deep gratitude. How many priests have been impeded from celebrating Mass for many years because of some sickness or infirmity. Now, the faculty to concelebrate, which is offered to them, brings a great consolation, namely the chance to exercise their priesthood again in that which is most proper to it : the offering of the sacrifice of the Body and Blood of the Lord.

The rules which have been worked out for this Ordo are characterized essentially by a very great flexibility :

> in the liturgical vestments required for concelebration (RC 142),
> in the choice of the concelebrants' position either at the beginning of the Mass (RC 143) or from the Offertory (RC 147),
> in standing or sitting (RC 143),
> in the recitation of the Proper and the Ordinary (RC 145),
> in the gestures which accompany the Canon (RC 150),
> in the kiss of peace (RC 152),
> in the choice of the Communion rite (RC 154).

Thus, the concelebration for priests who are infirm demands only two things : that the priests not be lying down (RC 140), and that each can recite with the other concelebrants the central part of the Canon, that is, from the *Hanc igitur* to the *Supplices te rogamus* inclusive (RC 150).

The description of the various forms of the concelebration rite, which began with the splendor of the liturgical assembly gathered around its Bishop, ends with the evocation of an image which could not be more evangelical.

Rite to be observed in the distribution of communion under both species

PRELIMINARY OBSERVATIONS

Those who may receive Communion under both species

1. The dogmatic principles laid down by the Council of Trent remaining intact, Communion under both species may be given in the following cases, according to the judgment of the Bishops :

1) to those ordained in the Mass of their Ordination;

2) to the deacon and subdeacon fulfilling their ministry in a Pontifical or solemn Mass;

3) to an abbess in the Mass of her Blessing;

4) to virgins in the Mass of their Consecration;

5) to the professed in the Mass of their religious Profession, if they profess their vows within the Mass;

6) to the spouses in their Nuptial Mass;

7) to newly-baptized adults in the Mass following their Baptism;

8) to adults confirmed in the Mass of their Confirmation;

9) to those already baptized, who are received into the communion of the Church;

10) to those mentioned in numbers 3 to 6, in the Mass of their jubilees;

11) to priests who are present at great celebrations and cannot celebrate or concelebrate; and to lay brothers who are present for concelebration in religious houses.

It is for the Bishop, in individual cases, to determine which of the described rites is to be used.

Commentary

The preface of this article reproduces the text of the conciliar Constitution authorizing the granting of Communion under both species : " The dogmatic principles which were laid down by the Council of Trent remaining intact, Communion under both species may be granted, according to the judgment of the Bishops, in the cases to be determined by the Apostolic See, not only to clerics and religious but also to the laity; for example : to the newly ordained in the Mass of their Ordination, to the professed in the Mass of their religious Profession, and to the newly baptized in the Mass that follows their Baptism " (C 55).

The Council has left it to the Bishops to decide when Communion under both species should be restored in each of the cases granted by the general law.   But as it also belongs to the Bishop to regulate " for his diocese, by his particular judgment, further determinations " in the celebration of the mysteries, [54] the Ritual of Communion gives him the faculty to choose in each case the rite to be used among those described in the present Ordo.

1.   *The Various Categories of Communicants*

In order to clarify the various categories of clerics and laymen admitted to the reception of Communion under both species, we present them here in an order different from that followed above.

Clerics

Three categories of clerics are allowed to receive Communion under both species :

Priests who assist at large celebrations and cannot celebrate or concelebrate.   Although the Council " strongly

---

[54] Decree *Christus Dominus* on the pastoral charge of Bishops, art. 15.

urges priests to celebrate Mass every day, " [55] there are cases in which it is impossible for them to do so, as for example in great celebrations where it would be difficult for each priest to celebrate fittingly because of the disproportion between the number of available altars and the number of celebrants. There is also the difficulty of concelebrating when the number of priests considerably exceeds a hundred. But, though the priests may not celebrate, it would be good that they participate in the meal of the Lord in its full sacramental signification.

Equally allowed to receive Communion under both species are priests who fulfill the functions of deacon or subdeacon in a concelebrated Mass. They may do so " even if they have already celebrated Mass or are going to celebrate " (RC 15). This favor is strictly bound to concelebration; it cannot be extended to any other Mass.

A deacon and subdeacon when they fulfill their ministry in a Pontifical or solemn Mass. For the Pontifical Mass, there is question of the deacon and subdeacon who serve the Bishop at the altar. Tradition has always considered them as members of the assembly who are most intimately associated with the Pontifical Mass; it is to them alone that the Bishop gives the kiss of peace after giving them the Body of Christ. The assisting deacons, the deacons who proclaim the Gospel in the various languages, and the subdeacon who carries the cross cannot be likened to them.

The sung Mass with deacon is assimilated to the solemn Mass (RC 77) and the deacon may receive Communion from the chalice.

Clerics newly ordained, in the Mass of their Ordination. Here there is question, as in the greater number of cases which follow, of Communion associated with the entrance into a new category of the Christian Community. The

---

[55] Decree *Presbyterorum Ordinis* on the ministry and life of priests, art. 13.

rule clearly concerns all the Orders, from the clerical Tonsure to the Diaconate.

Religious

Again here, three different circumstances can be distinguished in which religious may be allowed to receive Communion of the Blood of Christ :

In the Mass of their consecration to the Lord : the abbess who is blessed, the virgins who are consecrated according to the rite of the Roman Pontifical, the religious making their Profession. The text does not distinguish between simple and solemn Profession, but it requires that the act of Profession take place during the Mass.

In the Mass of their jubilees : these religious may be allowed to receive Communion under both species. By " jubilee " is to be understood the twenty-fifth and fiftieth anniversaries, but nothing prohibits local usages which also consider as jubilees the sixtieth anniversary or another occurrence.

Lay Brothers who assist at a concelebration in religious houses. Such a decision fully corresponds with the wish of the Council that " those who are called lay brothers, assistants, or some similar name should be drawn closely into the life and work of the community, in order that the members be more closely united by the bond of brotherly love. " [56] Now, the conventual Mass constitutes the most perfect work of the community, the *Opus Dei* par excellence. It is fitting, therefore, that the brothers be gathered intimately into the concelebration, in order that it may be both the sign and the source of the life of charity which should animate the total life of the community.

The general law places no limitation on the frequency of Communion under both species for lay brothers. If

---

[56] Decree *Perfectae caritatis* on the adapted renewal of religious life, art. 15.

there is a daily concelebration, then they may so receive
Communion every day. But there is a limitation concerning the place : the lay brothers may not receive
Communion of the Blood of the Lord at a concelebration
which takes place outside of their religious houses, for
example in a place of pilgrimage.

Communities do not include only priests and lay
brothers; ordinarily, there are choir novices and student
brothers who are preparing for the priesthood. Are these
to be the only ones excluded from the privilege of receiving
Communion from the chalice under the pretext that one
day they will celebrate Mass? The question extends also
to students of the major seminary who participate in the
concelebration of their professors. It is not for us to
give a larger interpretation to a text which is clear; but
it is greatly desired that this favor be granted in the future
by the competent authority.

The Laity

The laity may be allowed to receive Communion under
both kinds in the following circumstances :

*In the Mass of their Baptism and their Confirmation, if they
are adults, and in the Mass of their marriage.* The Ritual
says, " in the Mass which follows the Baptism " and " in the
Mass of the Confirmation and Marriage, " because Confirmation and Marriage are celebrated during the Mass,
after the homily, whereas, during the Paschal Vigil, the
Mass follows the Baptism. However, outside of the time
of Easter, there is no reason why Baptism cannot be
conferred on adults during the Mass, as is the case for
Confirmation and Marriage. Pope Paul VI himself baptized
twelve young Congolese at St. Paul-outside-the-Walls on
February 26, 1965. [57]

---

[57] *Beatissimus Pater, Eucharisticum sacrificium peragens, aliquot cate-
chumenos Congolenses sacro fonte lustravit, sacro chrismate unxit, ac divina
dape refecit,* AAS 57 (1965), p. 320.

It is easy to understand why Communion with the chalice has been granted as the completion of these three Sacraments : on the one hand, it completes the Christian initiation whose full development supposes the uninterrupted celebration of Baptism, Confirmation, and the Eucharist.   On the other hand, Marriage being a sign of the union of Christ and the Church, it is normal that it be sealed in the celebration of the Lord's Meal.   This is why the Gelasian Sacramentary, after giving the text for the nuptial blessing, adds : *Post haec dicis : Pax vobiscum. Et sic eos communicas.* [58] The *Pax vobiscum* was the invitation for the kiss of peace which the bridegroom received from the priest and which he gave to his bride. [59]

The exchange of a kiss in the midst of the liturgical assembly, and the participation in the Body and Blood of the Lord under the form of bread and the sharing of the same cup [60] : this was for a long time a sacred sign clearly manifesting the divine love which constitutes the marriage of two baptized people.

In the Mass of their marriage jubilee, the Christian spouses are again allowed to renew the " solemn Communion " which marked the beginning of their life together.

In the Mass in which those already baptized are received into the communion of the Church.   This Mass consecrates for them their admittance into the totality of the faith (*fidei integritas*) as the Liturgy of Good Friday expresses

---

[58] *Sacramentaire gélasien ancien*, ed. Mohlberg, *Liber sacramentorum romanae ecclesiae* (Rome : 1960), n⁰ 1453.

[59] The Roman Pontifical of the 12th century adds prudently : *Tunc subdiaconus dicit ad sponsum ut in ecclesia amplius cum ea pacem non faciat ;* ed. M. Andrieu, *op. cit.*, p. 302.

[60] The symbol of a cup shared between the new spouses is found in all civilizations : a cup of wine in Africa, a cup of milk and honey in the regions where Tamil is spoken (India), three cups in Japan.   See *Liturgie en mission, rapports et compte-rendu de la 33ᵉ semaine de missiologie, Louvain* 1963 (Desclée de Brouwer 1964), pp. 142, 155 and 259.

it. [61]   Communion in the Blood of Christ is even more meaningful for these Christians who often have behind them a long practice of Communion under both kinds. Yet, their first Communion in the Catholic Church is likewise their last Communion with the chalice.

There is a final situation in which many priests, clerics, religious and faithful would like to receive Communion in the Body and Blood of the Lord : it is at the moment of death, when they receive Viaticum. The Ritual makes no allusion to it. It is to be hoped that one day, this usage, so profoundly traditional, will be reborn in the Western Church.

Perhaps, on certain occasions, the faculty to receive Communion from the chalice will also be extended to determined groups of the faithful. This was done on March 27, 1966, when the Pope permitted a group of young university students of Rome to receive their Easter Communion under both kinds. [62]

2.   *Ways of Receiving Communion under Both Species*

The Ritual allows different ways of receiving Communion under both species as we have already encountered in our study of concelebration : Communion directly from the chalice, Communion from the chalice with a straw or spoon, and Communion by intinction. But, just as it belongs to the Bishops to decide if they will restore in their dioceses Communion under both species for each of the categories foreseen by the general law, so also they have the power " to choose in each case the rite to be used. "

---

[61] Roman Missal, Office of Good Friday, Prayer of the Faithful, prayer n° 7.

[62] *L'Avvenire d'Italia* of March 27, 1966.

Catechetical Preparation

2. Pastors of souls are to see to it that the faithful who participate in this rite, or who are present for it, are instructed in the best way possible regarding the Catholic doctrine concerning Holy Communion according to the Council of Trent (Session XXI, 1-3). They should strive especially to teach the Catholic doctrine that even " under only one kind, Christ, whole and entire, and the true sacrament, is received, and, moreover, regarding its fruits, no grace necessary for salvation is denied those who receive under only one kind " (ibid., c. 3).

They are also to explain that the Church, in administering the sacraments, has the power, in virtue of varying circumstances, times and places, to regulate and change, not the substance of the sacraments, but whatever she judges would bring about a greater reverence for the sacraments and the greater welfare of those who receive them (cf. ibid., c. 2). At the same time, however, pastors should urge the faithful to participate in this sacred rite which brings to light more thoroughly the signification of the Eucharistic banquet.

Commentary

The catechetical preparation for Communion under both species is not only meant for the faithful who will so receive Communion, but also for everyone who will assist at the rite, for the conciliar Constitution wishes that the rites be adapted to the understanding of all the faithful present (C 34). These rites should never provoke surprise or be a matter of simple curiosity. [63]

The present article is not content simply to order a catechesis of Communion from the chalice, but further formulates its content as deriving from the teaching of the Council of Trent and the Second Vatican Council.

---

[63] This is why the French Episcopate has been careful to permit this form of Communion to spouses at their Nuptial Mass only if the assembly is prepared to understand the signification of the rite and its sacred value.

The Council of Trent, following the Council of Constance, has defined that Christ is integrally present under each of the sacramental species and it has drawn the conclusion that " no grace necessary for salvation is refused to those who receive only under one kind " (above, p. 56). In other words, the same Christ is received as fully by those receiving Communion only with the bread as by those receiving Communion successively with the bread and the chalice.

But the Council of Trent has also defined that " in the dispensation of the sacraments, their substance being preserved, the Church has always possessed the power to decree or modify that which she judges more in accord with the benefit of those who receive the sacraments or with the respect due to the sacraments, according to varying times and places " (c. 2). The argument formulated in 1562 to explain how the Western Church was able legitimately to abandon the usage of giving the chalice to the faithful is such that it can be used in 1965 to justify the restoration of an earlier tradition. This is not a subtle juggling, but rather a just appreciation of what is immutable in the Christian cult and what is subject to change (C 21).

Why did the Second Vatican Council introduce a change so important? The Council acted thus because it was sensible to the fact that Communion under both species " brings to light more thoroughly the signification of the Eucharistic banquet. " This results from its doctrine on the sacraments which underlines the nature of signs : " As signs they also instruct. They not only suppose the faith, but *by words and objects* they also nourish, strengthen and express it " (C 59). The Eucharist is the " paschal banquet " (C 47) and it is fitting that at the most important times of their life, all the faithful be able to participate at this banquet in the full sign of a meal.

But, if Communion from the chalice supposes a preliminary catechesis, it does not require a more ascetical preparation than Communion only under the kind of bread. The Council has reserved Communion from the chalice for the faithful to special circumstances; it has not made it a privilege for fervent Christians. To think, for example, that certain ones are worthy to receive Communion under both species for their marriage jubilee, whereas others should be content to receive Communion in the usual manner would be to fall into a grave doctrinal error. This would be to think that the sacraments are rewards for human virtue, whereas " their purpose is to sanctify men " (C 59), and to allow it to be thought that the fruit of the sacrament is more abundant when it is received under both species. And this, indeed, is precisely the error against which the Council of Trent warned.

Preparations

3. For distributing Communion under both species, the following articles are to be prepared :

a) If Communion from the chalice is to be taken with a straw, silver straws for the celebrant and for the individual communicants, and a container with water for purifying the straws.

b) If the Precious Blood is administered with a spoon, one spoon.

c) If Communion under both species is to be distributed by dipping the Host in the Precious Blood, provision must be made that the hosts are not too thin nor too small, and a little thicker than usual so that when they are partially dipped in the Precious Blood, they conveniently be distributed.

Commentary

Since Communion under both species is always given within the Mass, the prescriptions which are here formulated are only a repetition of certain paragraphs of article 17 of the Ritual of concelebration. They concern the straw and the spoon (RC 17 g) as well as the Hosts for Communion by intinction (RC 17 c). It might have been necessary to also anticipate, as in the case of concelebration (RC 17 d), the possibility of using many chalices on those occasions when the communicants would be numerous (for example, an Ordination or a religious Profession).

1. *RITE OF COMMUNION UNDER BOTH SPECIES WHEN THE COMMUNICANTS DRINK FROM THE CHALICE ITSELF*

If there is a deacon or another priest

4. If there is a deacon or another priest to assist him :

a) the celebrant receives the Body and Blood of the Lord in the usual way, seeing to it that enough of the Precious Blood remain in the chalice for the communicants; he wipes the outside of the chalice with a purificator.

b) the celebrant hands the chalice with a purificator to the deacon, and he himself takes a paten or ciborium with the Hosts. Standing, and facing the people, with the deacon at his right holding the chalice, he says Ecce Agnus Dei, and the communicants add the threefold Domine non sum dignus; then the celebrant and the deacon stand where it is most convenient to give Communion to the faithful.

c) each communicant comes forward, genuflects, and stands before the celebrant. The celebrant, elevating the Host, says Corpus Christi, to which the communicant replies Amen and he receives the Body of the Lord from the celebrant.

d) the communicant then goes to the deacon and stands before him. The deacon says Sanguis Christi, to which the communicant replies Amen; the deacon holds out the purificator and the chalice, which the communicant, in order to drink conveniently, brings with his hands to his mouth. The communicant, with his left hand holding the purificator under his mouth, and careful not to spill any of the Precious Blood, drinks a little from the chalice, and then leaves; the deacon then wipes the outside of the chalice with the purificator.

e) If there are others present who are to receive only under the one kind, the deacon places the chalice on the altar after all those who are to receive under both species have drunk from the chalice. The celebrant, however, gives Communion to the faithful, and then returns to the altar. He, or the deacon, consumes what remains of the Precious Blood, and he takes the purifications as usual.

Commentary

The first thing to be noted is the priority given to the deacon as minister of the Precious Blood, this conforming to the most ancient and universal tradition (above, p. 48). From this description of the rite, three points should be remembered.

The faithful receive the Body of Christ standing.   This is the first time that a recent liturgical document prescribes this position.   No doubt, this has been done because of a particular situation, but it is legitimate to take this as a way of organizing habitually the Communion procession, especially when the communicants are numerous.   The Ritual specifies that each communicant " makes a genuflection. "   In all places where it is the practice to receive Communion standing, it would be fitting to establish a rite of adoration.   However, a profound bow, which is the practice of the Oriental Christians, might be preferred to a genuflection.   It seems that this form of venerating the Holy Eucharist was practiced in France up to the eighteenth century, especially by women.

The communicant himself takes the chalice in his hands " in order to drink conveniently. "   This should be made very clear before the Mass to those who are going to communicate.   The faithful have been taught to have a great respect toward the sacred species and the sacred vessels, and this might make them hesitate before a very natural and simple gesture which consists in taking the cup **in** their own hands to bring it to their lips.

After giving Communion from the chalice, the deacon may allow the celebrant to consume the remainder of the sacred wine and take the ablutions, or he may do it himself, as at concelebration (RC 52). The latter method is preferable, since the ablutions and the purification of the chalice are simple material functions and it would be better to free the celebrant of these things as much as possible.

If the celebrant is alone

5. If there is no deacon or other priest :

a) the celebrant receives the Body and Blood of the Lord in the usual way, seeing to it that enough of the Precious Blood remain in the chalice for the communicants; he wipes the outside of the chalice with a purificator.

b) the celebrant says the Ecce Agnus Dei as usual, and the communicants add the threefold Domine non sum dignus; then the celebrant stands where it is most convenient to give Communion, and he gives the Body of the Lord in the usual way to the communicants who are to receive under both species; they come forward, genuflect, and stand before the celebrant, and after receiving the Body of the Lord, they stand back a little.

c) When all the communicants have received the Body of the Lord, the celebrant puts the ciborium on the altar and he takes up the chalice and a purificator. Those who are to receive Communion from the chalice come forward again one by one, genuflect, and stand before him. The celebrant says Sanguis Christi and the communicant replies Amen; the celebrant holds out the chalice and the purificator. The communicant, with his left hand holding the purificator under his mouth, and careful not to spill any of the Precious Blood, drinks a little from the chalice, and then leaves. The celebrant wipes the outside of the chalice with the purificator.

d) After the Communion from the chalice has been completed, the celebrant places the chalice on the altar, and if there are others to receive Communion under only one kind, he gives the Communion in the usual way. Afterwards, he returns to the altar, consumes what remains of the Precious Blood, and takes the purifications as usual.

2.   *RITE OF COMMUNION*
UNDER BOTH SPECIES BY INTINCTION

If there is a deacon or another priest

6.   If there is a deacon or another priest to assist him :

a) the celebrant hands him the chalice with a purificator, and he himself takes the paten or ciborium with the Hosts. Standing, and facing the people, with the deacon at his left holding the chalice, he says Ecce Agnus Dei and the communicants add the threefold Domine non sum dignus; then the celebrant and the deacon stand where they can most conveniently give Communion.

b) the communicants come forward one by one; each genuflects and, holding a paten under his mouth, stands before the celebrant.   The celebrant dips a part of the Host in the chalice and elevating it says Corpus et Sanguis Christi, to which the communicant replies Amen.   He receives Communion from the celebrant and leaves.

c) the Communion of others who are to receive under only one kind, the consuming of the Precious Blood that remains, and the purifications are carried out as explained above.

Commentary

The deacon is no longer the minister of the Blood of Christ in this form of Communion under both species. He only holds the chalice in his hands, while the celebrant dips the consecrated bread in the chalice and pronounces the words which accompany the showing of the sacred species to each communicant.

If the celebrant is alone

7.   If there is no deacon or other priest :

a) the celebrant, after he receives the Precious Blood, takes the paten or ciborium with the Hosts between the index and middle finger of his left hand and the chalice between the thumb and index finger of the same hand and, standing facing the people, he says Ecce Agnus Dei and the communicants add the threefold Domine non sum dignus;

then the celebrant stands where he can most conveniently give Communion.

b) the communicants come forward one by one; each genuflects and, holding a paten under his mouth, stands before the celebrant. The celebrant dips a part of the Host in the chalice and elevating it says Corpus et Sanguis Christi to which the communicant replies Amen. He receives Communion from the celebrant and leaves.

c) It is also permissible to place on the bottom step of the altar or at the sanctuary gates a small table covered with a cloth and corporal on which the celebrant may put the chalice, so that it will be easier for him to distribute Communion.

d) the Communion of others who are to receive under only one kind, the consuming of the Precious Blood which remains, and the purifications are carried out as explained above.

Commentary

The redactors of this article have furnished a great deal of clarity in their description of a very complicated rite. First of all, it is not easy to hold the chalice and paten in the same hand, and yet, neither is it very esthetic to place the chalice on a small table in order to more conveniently dip the consecrated bread. The concrete difficulty which Communion by intinction presents when the celebrant is alone is enough to lead one to prefer, in this case, another manner of Communion with the Precious Blood.

3. *RITE OF COMMUNION UNDER BOTH SPECIES WITH A STRAW*

8. The celebrant also uses the straw to receive the Precious Blood.

Commentary

When he is going to give Communion with a straw, the celebrant himself also communicates with the straw. For, it would be contrary to the law to prepare two chalices, one from which the celebrant would drink directly and another from which the other communicants would drink with a straw.

If there is a deacon or another priest

9.　If there is a deacon or another priest :

a) for receiving the Body of the Lord in Communion, all is done as explained above in number 4, b and c.

b) the communicant then goes to the deacon and stands before him.　The deacon says Sanguis Christi and the communicant replies Amen.　He then takes a straw from an acolyte and places it into the chalice and drinks a little of the Precious Blood.　He then takes out the straw, careful not to let drop any of the Precious Blood, and he places the straw in a container of water which an acolyte or server, standing by the deacon, holds in his hands; drawing and drinking a little of the water, he thus purifies the straw and places it in a container held out to him by the acolyte.

Commentary

The deacon fulfills his role as minister of the Blood of Christ in this form of Communion from the chalice, since he says the formula *the Blood of Christ* to each communicant.

It is not specified here that there should be as many straws as communicants, but this is mentioned explicitly in the concelebration rite (RC 17 g) and the straws are also spoken of in article 3 as among the objects to be prepared (DC 3).

If the celebrant is alone

10.　If there is no deacon or another priest, the celebrant himself offers the chalice to each of the communicants, in the order described above (art. 5) for Communion from the chalice, and an acolyte or server standing beside him holds a container of water for purifying the straw.

4. *RITE OF COMMUNION*
UNDER BOTH SPECIES WITH A SPOON

If there is a deacon or another priest

11. If there is a deacon or another priest to assist the celebrant, he himself holds the chalice in his left hand, and with a spoon, and careful not to touch their lips or tongue with it, distributes the Precious Blood to the communicants, saying Sanguis Christi; each communicant holds a paten under his mouth while receiving.

Commentary

The rite of Communion with a spoon is not at all the same for the concelebrants and for other communicants. In a concelebrated Mass, the concelebrants proceed " in the same way as for receiving Communion with a straw " (RC 55), that is, they take a spoon in their hands and dip it themselves in the chalice to draw out the Precious Blood. Each one has an individual spoon.

In the rite described here, it is the deacon who draws out the Precious Blood with a spoon and puts it in the mouth of each communicant, being careful not to touch the communicant's lips or tongue. Obviously, he uses only one spoon. One can easily recognize here a practice fairly well known in the East. But, it is not easy to place in the mouth of the communicant some wine without the risk of some inconvenience for him or the spilling of some drops of the Precious Blood on the paten. Communion of the faithful with a spoon, therefore, does not seem destined to be widely used.

If the celebrant is alone

12. If there is no deacon or another priest, the celebrant himself, after distributing the Body of the Lord to all who are to receive Communion under both species, also distributes the Precious Blood to each of them.

3

CANON OF THE MASS
FOR CONCELEBRATION

The principal celebrant alone sings the dialogue before the Preface to which all respond, and the Preface itself. But, the *Sanctus* is sung by all the concelebrants together with the people and the choir.

After the chant, the concelebrants continue the Canon in the manner indicated below.

However, only the principal celebrant makes the gestures, unless otherwise indicated.

The *Te igitur* is said aloud by the principal celebrant alone.

The principal celebrant, extending, raising and joining his hands, and lifting up his eyes and lowering them immediately, bowing deeply before the altar with his hands placed on it, says aloud :

Te ígitur, clementíssime Pater,
Per Iesum Christum, Fílium tuum, Dóminum nostrum,
súpplices rogámus ac pétimus,

he kisses the altar and, with hands joined, he says :

uti accépta hábeas et benedícas

he makes the sign of the cross three times over the Host and chalice together, saying :

hæc ✝ dona,
hæc ✝ múnera,
hæc ✝ sancta sacrifícia illibáta,

with his hands extended he continues :

in primis, quæ tibi offérimus
pro ecclésia tua sancta cathólica :
quam pacificáre, custodíre, adunáre et régere dignéris
toto orbe terrárum :
una cum fámulo tuo Papa nostro N.
et Antístite nostro N.
et ómnibus orthodóxis atque cathólicæ et apostólicæ
fídei cultóribus.

Commemoration of the living

The principal celebrant may commission one of the concelebrants to say the *Memento* of the living, in which case he alone with his hands extended says this prayer aloud.

Meménto, Dómine, famulórum famularúmque tuárum N. et N.

He joins his hands, and all pray a little while for those for whom they wish to pray;
then, the same concelebrating priest, with his hands extended, continues :

et ómnium circumstántium,
quorum tibi fides cógnita est et nota devótio,
pro quibus tibi offérimus :
vel qui tibi ófferunt hoc sacrifícium laudis,
pro se suísque ómnibus :
pro redemptióne animárum suárum,
pro spe salútis et incolumitátis suæ :
tibíque reddunt vota sua
ætérno Deo,

he joins his hands

vivo et vero.

Within the sacred action

The principal celebrant may commission one of the concelebrants to say the *Communicantes*, in which case he alone with his hands extended says this prayer aloud.

Communicántes,
et memóriam venerántes,
in primis gloriósæ semper Vírginis Maríæ,
Genetrícis Dei et Dómini nostri Iesu Christi :
sed et beáti Ioseph, eiúsdem Vírginis Sponsi,
et beatórum Apostolórum ac Mártyrum tuórum,
Petri et Pauli,

Andréæ, Iacóbi, Ioánnis,
Thomæ, Iacóbi, Philíppi,
Bartholomǽi, Matthǽi,
Simónis et Thaddǽi :
Lini, Cleti,
Cleméntis, Xysti,
Cornélii, Cypriáni,
Lauréntii, Chrysógoni,
Ioánnis et Pauli,
Cosmæ et Damiáni :
et ómnium Sanctórum tuórum;
quorum méritis precibúsque concédas,
ut in ómnibus protectiónis tuæ muniámur auxílio.

He joins his hands

Per eúndem Christum Dóminum nostrum.
Amen.

From the *Hanc igitur* to the *Supplices* inclusive, all the concelebrants together chant all the words or recite them aloud :

Hanc ígitur oblatiónem servitútis nostræ,
sed et cunctæ famíliæ tuæ,
quǽsumus, Dómine, ut placátus accípias :
diésque nostros in tua pace dispónas,
atque ab ætérna damnatióne nos éripi
et in electórum tuórum iúbeas grege numerári.

All fold their hands.

Per Christum Dóminum nostrum. Amen.

And, with hands folded, all continue :

Quam oblatiónem tu, Deus, in ómnibus, quǽsumus,

the principal celebrant makes the sign of the cross three times over the offerings,

bene + díctam,
adscríp + tam,
ra + tam,
rationábilem, acceptabilémque fácere dignéris :

he makes the sign of the cross once over the Host,

ut nobis Cor + pus

et once over the chalice,

et San + guis fiat dilectíssimi Fílii tui,

he joins his hands,

Dómini nostri Iesu Christi.
Qui prídie quam paterétur

the principal celebrant takes the Host,

accépit panem in sanctas ac venerábiles manus suas,

he raises his eyes,

et elevátis óculis in cælum
ad te Deum Patrem suum omnipoténtem,

all bow their heads,

tibi grátias agens,

the principal celebrant makes the sign of the cross over
the Host,

bene + díxit,
fregit,
dedítque discípulis suis, dicens :
Accípite, et manducáte ex hoc omnes.

The principal celebrant holds the Host in both hands
between his index fingers and thumbs. All pronounce
the words of Consecration distinctly and attentively over
the Host, and at the same time over all the Hosts, if there
are others to be consecrated. The concelebrants, however,
extend their right hand toward the bread, if this seems
suitable.

Hoc est enim Corpus meum.

After these words are said, the principal celebrant
immediately genuflects and adores the consecrated Host.
He rises, shows it to the people, replaces it upon the
corporal, and genuflecting, adores it again. He does not
separate his thumbs and index fingers again, except when
touching the Host, until he washes his fingers.

While the principal celebrant elevates the Host, the concelebrants look at it; and then, when the principal celebrant genuflects again, they bow deeply.

Then, when the chalice is uncovered, all say :
Símili modo postquam cenátum est,

the principal celebrant takes the chalice in both hands,
accípiens et hunc præclárum cálicem
in sanctas ac venerábiles manus suas :

all bow their heads,
item tibi grátias agens,

the principal celebrant, holding the chalice with his left hand, makes the sign of the cross over it with his right hand,
bene + díxit,
dedítque discípulis suis, dicens :
Accípite, et bíbite ex eo omnes.

The principal celebrant holds the chalice raised a little. All pronounce the words of Consecration over the chalice attentively and in a continued manner. The concelebrants, however, while pronouncing the words of Consecration, extend their right hand toward the chalice, if this seems suitable.
Hic est enim Calix Sánguinis mei,
novi et ætérni testaménti :
mystérium fídei :
qui pro vobis et pro multis effundétur
in remissiónem peccatórum.

After these words have been spoken, the principal celebrant places the chalice upon the corporal, and all say :
Hæc quotiescúmque fecéritis,
in mei memóriam faciétis.

The principal celebrant genuflects in adoration; he rises, shows the chalice to the people, replaces it on the corporal, covers it, and genuflects in adoration.

While the principal celebrant raises the chalice, the concelebrants look at it; and then, when the principal celebrant genuflects again, they bow deeply.

With hands extended, all the concelebrants chant or say aloud :

Unde et mémores, Dómine,
nos servi tui,
sed et plebs tua sancta,
eiúsdem Christi Fílii tui, Dómini nostri,
tam beátæ passiónis,
nec non et ab ínferis resurrectiónis,
sed et in cælos gloriósæ ascensiónis :
offérimus præcláræ maiestáti tuæ
de tuis donis ac datis

the principal celebrant joins his hands, and then makes the sign of the cross three times over the Host and chalice together,

hóstiam + puram,
hóstiam + sanctam,
hóstiam + immaculátam,

he makes the sign of the cross once over the Host,

Panem + sanctum vitæ ætérnæ

and once over the chalice

et Cálicem + salútis perpétuæ.

Then, with hands extended, all continue together :

Supra quæ propítio ac seréno vultu respícere dignéris :
et accépta habére,
sícuti accépta habére dignátus es
múnera púeri tui iusti Abel,
et sacrifícium Patriárchæ nostri Abrahæ :
et quod tibi óbtulit summus sacérdos tuus Melchísedech,
sanctum sacrifícium, immaculátam hóstiam.

Bowing deeply, with hands folded, all say :

Súpplices te rogámus, omnípotens Deus :
iube hæc perférri per manus sancti Angeli tui in sublíme
altáre tuum,

in conspéctu divínæ maiestátis tuæ;
ut, quotquot

the principal celebrant and the concelebrants who are standing around the altar mensa, kiss it; then all stand erect,

ex hac altáris participatióne
sacrosánctum Fílii tui

they fold their hands, and the principal celebrant makes the sign of the cross once over the Host, and once over the chalice,

Cor + pus
et Sán + guinem sumpsérimus,

all sign themselves,

omni benedictióne cælésti et grátia repleámur.

all join their hands

Per eúndem Christum Dóminum nostrum.
Amen.

Commemoratio of the dead

The principal celebrant may commission one of the concelebrants to say the *Memento* of the dead, in which case he alone with his hands extended says this prayer aloud.

Meménto étiam, Dómine, famulórum famularúmque tuárum
N. et N.,
qui nos præcessérunt cum signo fídei,
et dórmiunt in somno pacis.

He joins his hands, and all pray a little while for the dead for whom they wish to pray. Then, with hands extended, the same concelebrant continues :

Ipsis, Dómine, et ómnibus in Christo quiescéntibus,
locum refrigérii, lucis et pacis,
ut indúlgeas, deprecámur.

He joins his hands, saying :
Per eúndem Christum Dóminum nostrum.
Amen.

The principal celebrant may commission one of the concelebrants to say the *Nobis quoque peccatoribus*, in which case he alone, with his hands extended, says this prayer aloud.

At the words *Nobis quoque peccatoribus*, all the concelebrants strike their breast.

Nobis quoque peccatóribus

With his hands extended, the concelebrant continues :
fámulis tuis,
de multitúdine miseratiónum tuárum sperántibus,
partem áliquam et societátem donáre dignéris,
cum tuis sanctis Apóstolis et Martýribus :
cum Ioánne, Stéphano,
Matthía, Bárnaba,
Ignátio, Alexándro,
Marcellíno, Petro,
Felicitáte, Perpétua,
Agatha, Lúcia,
Agnéte, Cæcília, Anastásia,
et ómnibus Sanctis tuis :
intra quorum nos consórtium,
non æstimátor mériti,
sed véniæ, quæsumus, largítor admítte.

He folds his hands.
Per Christum Dóminum nostrum.

Only the principal celebrant says :
Per quem hæc ómnia, Dómine,
semper bona creas,

he makes the sign of the cross three times over the Host and chalice together, saying :
sanctí ✝ ficas,
viví ✝ ficas,
bene ✝ dícis
et præstas nobis.

The principal celebrant uncovers the chalice, genuflects, takes the Host between the thumb and index finger of his right hand, and the chalice in his left hand; he elevates the chalice a little, with the Host held over it, and together with all the concelebrants he chants or says aloud :

**Per ipsum, et cum ipso, et in ipso,
est tibi Deo Patri omnipoténti,
in unitáte Spíritus Sancti,
omnis honor et glória,
per ómnia sæcula sæculórum.**

All respond : **Amen.**

N⁰ 173. — Printed in Belgium by Desclée & Co., Éditeurs, S. A. Tournai — 10.843
D - 1967 - 0002 - 11